TALES *from a* FREE-RANGE CHILDHOOD

JOHN F. BLAIR, PUBLISHER
WINSTON-SALEM, NORTH CAROLINA

TALES *from a* FREE-RANGE CHILDHOOD

Donald Davis

JOHN F. BLAIR
PUBLISHER

1406 Plaza Drive
Winston-Salem, North Carolina 27103
www.blairpub.com

Copyright © 2011 by Donald Davis

Manufactured in the United States of America

COVER PHOTO BY DONALD'S FATHER, JOE DAVIS,
WHO LOVED TO TAKE PICTURES WITH HIS KODAK 616 BOX CAMERA

Library of Congress Cataloging-in-Publication Data

Davis, Donald, 1944-
  Tales from a free-range childhood / by Donald Davis.
    p.   cm.
  ISBN 978-0-89587-507-5 (hardcover : alk. paper)—ISBN 978-0-89587-509-9 (pbk. : alk. paper)- —ISBN 978-0-89587-508-2 (ebook) 1. Davis, Donald, 1944—Childhood and youth. 2. North Carolina—Social life and customs. 3. Authors, American—20th century--Biography. 4. Davis, Donald, 1944- —Family. I. Title.
  PS3554.A93347Z475 2011
  813'.54—dc22
  [B]
                                        2010051339

Design by Debra Long Hampton

For Thomas D. D.

CONTENTS

AUTHOR'S NOTE

For more than thirty years, I have traveled as a performing storyteller. The stories that I tell are my own, built from reflections upon personal experiences and a lifetime of memories. They are put together to work first in a setting of telling with a live audience and, as such, are created in an oral/kinesthetic process without text. No writing is done until I know how the story "goes," how it works, and all of the ins and outs of telling with various audiences and various time requirements.

The stories in this collection are in that sense not "new." They are part of the total canon of stories that I have been telling, some for years. Two things bring them into print now. First, they have now matured to the point at which I feel comfortable documenting a written version for readers whom I shall perhaps never meet and who can ask no questions for unresolved clarity. Second, none of them have been previously published.

They are built of childhood memories, seen through one teller's eyes but told with certain belief that others who were there would not fail to have parallel memories. I have arranged them in the order of their chronological ending places, so the whole may have a more integrated memoir feel than in a set of unconnected stories.

My hope is always that they will serve as memory dusters for readers, and that readers will end up telling stories of their own about which they would not have thought without reading these.

Chapter 1

WATCH THE BABY

eing the firstborn child in our household and the first grandson in Mama's entire extended family, I experienced early confusion about exactly what my name was supposed to be. When you are a child, you do not learn your name by reading it on your birth certificate. No, you infer your intended label by the repeated observation of what you happen to be called by those adults (or available children) whom you happen to trust.

According to this process, I soon determined that my given name was Baby! After all, that was the constant oral label placed upon me by Mama, Daddy, and even my trustworthy grandmother. After all, I was the first (in our family) baby.

In case anyone without this experience wonders, it is important to know that Baby is not a bad name. No, it is in fact a very good name. When your name is Baby, you get to do exactly whatever you want to do! It was spoiling and wonderful!

I got along very well being the singular family Baby for nearly three years. But when the unanticipated arrival of my little brother interfered with the established order of things, even my name changed. Suddenly, everyone started calling me Donald. And my old, dear name, Baby, went to my uninvited (by me) little brother.

People came to see him in droves. Their assessment was always the same: "Look at that beautiful baby! He is so gorgeous!" My disgust was profound.

When I stop to think about it, the real trouble with having a little brother was not with the fact of his personal existence. No, I did not actually mind his presence at all. In fact, the first thing I did when he came home from the hospital was to admire and kiss him. No, the problem was that he interfered with my already busy life.

As a child, I was very involved in scientific inquiry. Each day was filled with educational experiments in my early effort to put the world in controllable order. My realization was that parents simply refused to tell you things that you need to know (example: "Do you think that my broken dump truck will flush down the toilet?"), which led to a constant life of scientific experimentation. This is where the little brother problem came into the mix.

I would be right in the middle of an educational scientific experiment when suddenly my mama would arrive. "There you are!" was her normal announcement. "I was looking for you." Then something like this would follow: "I need to go out in the yard and hang out the clothes. You come in the house and watch the baby."

I was unbelievably amazed as I stared back at her. *You,* I thought, *are an adult woman, and you cannot see that I am busy! I do not have time to watch your baby. You wanted the little thing. I guess you can watch it!* Of course, these words were thought and never actually spoken.

"Come on, now, you are my only little helper. Come in the house and watch the baby!"

Okay, I thought. *I will watch the baby. Maybe someone will come to the door, and they can have him!* I simply hated to stop my important work to watch the baby.

I had a cousin named Andy. Andy and I were born less than a year apart. I happened to get here first, but he was close behind me. Most people understood Andy and me very clearly: since we were cousins and not brothers, we liked one another! I would go to his house and spend the day playing. He would come to my house and spend the day playing. Either way, we were happy!

One day, Andy's mama, my aunt Eddie, had to go somewhere for the day. So the plan was made for her to bring him over to our house, where he would play with me until she got back.

When they arrived, Andy had brought a basket that was filled with his little cars and trucks. When I saw that, I added enough of my own little cars and trucks to fill the basket to the rim. With these toys in hand, we told his mama goodbye and headed out the back door and across the yard to the corner of my daddy's garden. There were four things there that we needed: dirt, tools for digging, the water hose, and . . . it was out of sight of my mama!

Andy and I worked very hard. We dug the dirt loose, turned on the water hose, mixed and stirred. Pretty soon, we had created a gigantic and gorgeous pit of mud. Now we could use the mud like it was asphalt and build little roads all over the backyard that could then bake in the hot sun and be smooth and hard for our little cars and trucks. It really was hard work. When we first got out there, there was grass we had to get rid of before we could even begin to do anything.

All of a sudden, our work was disturbed. It was Mama coming

to look for us. "There you are, boys! I need you! I need to go back in the garden and pick some beans for our supper. Andy, you and Eddie will probably stay and eat with us before you go home tonight. So I need for you boys to go in the house and watch the baby while I am out in the garden."

Andy looked up at Mama and announced, "We are busy!"

"Not anymore, you're not," she replied. "Now, you boys go on in the house and watch the baby."

My cousin Andy was only five years old, but he already had developed a totally functional little smart mouth. He was not to be stopped. "I have a question." He was looking straight at Mama.

"What's your question, sweetheart?" Mama was patient with him.

"What I want to know is, what do you have to do around here to get fired?"

"What do you mean, 'get fired'?" Her patience was wearing a little now.

"I'll tell you what I mean." Andy dug deeper. "What do you have to do around here to get fired from watching a baby?"

"Mister," she called Andy, and it wasn't even his name, "you just get that out of your little mind. You cannot get fired from watching a baby. There is no one else around here to watch him. Besides"—she was looking at both of us now—"both of you boys know deep in your hearts that you love him!"

Andy and I were trying hard not to gag on that one. "Now"— she was talking with her finger wagging at us—"get . . . in . . . the . . . house . . . and . . . watch . . . the . . . baby!"

We had no choice. As she headed to the garden, Andy and I started to the house.

Just inside the kitchen, we found my brother, Joe, playing in his playpen. It was not a new playpen with silvery chrome pipes and little padded meshlike stuff around the sides. No, it was an old-fashioned, square, wooden playpen, the kind that had wooden bars. It looked exactly like a jailhouse for babies!

Andy and I studied Joe for a minute, trying to decide exactly what we had to do to "watch" him.

All of a sudden, we both had the same realization at the same time: Mama was way out in the garden where she could not hear us! So we decided to play our favorite game: Make the Baby Cry.

It was a good game. We played it with cookies.

Andy and I got the big jar of cookies down off the kitchen cabinet. We then sat there on the floor and watched Joe watch us eat cookies! His little arms would come through the bars of the playpen as he reached toward us, begging, "Aaaaah! I want a cookie! Aaaaah!" He reached so far that his face was mashed against the bars.

We would hold a cookie out to him and hold it closer and closer until he could almost touch the cookie. Then we would pull it back and eat it ourselves. He cried every time. It was wonderful.

Pretty soon, all the cookies were gone and we had to play another game. We called the new game "Fishing for Babies."

Joe would periodically drop one of his toys out of the playpen or accidentally lose a toy out through the bars. He then wanted us to pick up the toy and toss it back in to him. We would pick up the toy. But before we tossed it back, we would tie a long piece of string to it. Then, holding our end of the string, we would launch the toy back toward Joe in the playpen. When he tried to grab it, Andy and I would jerk the other end of the string. We did this over and over again, just like trying to hook a trout! It was great fun for all three of us. Joe laughed so much (especially when we called him a fish) that he forgot about the entire cookie business.

Finally, we were tired of that. "Play with your toys," I ordered

Joe. "Play with your toys and stop bothering us."

He did not agree. "Aaaaah, play with me, play with me!" Joe wailed.

"Hush!" I countered his noise. "Play with your toys. You have plenty of toys. I know what. Play 'Punching Bag' with your little rattle. I'll fix it for you."

One of Joe's favorite little toys was a rattle that had originally belonged to me. It was a rattle that was very popular in those days but disappeared from the market as soon as child safety was invented.

The rattle was like a plastic clown's head, slightly smaller than a tennis ball. It was hollow with something like dried beans or BBs inside so it would rattle. But instead of having a handle like most baby rattles, it was different. Right where the clown's neck would logically be, there was fastened a metal spring. The spring was very flexible and about four or five inches long. At its bottom end, there was attached a large rubber suction cup. The idea was that the suction cup could be stuck to places like the baby's high-chair tray or the kitchen tabletop, and you could bat the little clown around, watch the head dance, and listen to the rattle. Joe loved it.

One day, our daddy had come walking into the kitchen when Joe was on the floor playing with the rattle. Daddy had picked up the rattle, licked the suction cup, and stuck it sideways on the lower kitchen cabinet door. "Now"—he pointed to the rattle as he informed Joe—"you have a punching bag! See? Go over there and knock its head off!"

Joe really loved it now. He went over to the quivering clown's head, and all afternoon he punched it back and forth—*Pow, pow, pow!* It was great.

Now, Andy and I were ready to fix the rattle so Joe could

again have his punching bag. We pushed the playpen across the floor until one barred side was flush against the bottom cabinet door. I picked up the rattle, reached through the bars, and stuck it onto the cabinet. "Now," I instructed, "punching bag!"

Joe crawled over to the rattle. *Pow!* went his little two-year-old fist. The rattle immediately fell off the cabinet door.

I realized what the problem was. I had forgotten to wet the rubber suction cup. So I picked up the rattle from where it had landed on the floor, licked it all over, and reached back to stick it again.

That's when Andy got his good idea. (From here on, everything was his fault.) "Stick it on his head!" he suggested.

So we used the best flat place we could find: his forehead. We stuck that slobbery suction cup right in the center of Joe's forehead as firmly as we possibly could.

It was fabulous! The little clown stuck out from Joe's forehead like he was a unicorn. When he moved his head, it swayed back and forth. He batted it alternately with his hands, at the same time shaking his head and laughing. Andy and I were out of control, rolling on the floor and laughing until tears came out of our eyes. This was the best thing we had ever done!

My brother, Joe, thought that the stuck rattle was funny for all of about two minutes. Then it started to hurt. He began to whimper, "Get it off, get it off!" Then his sound accelerated to a cry: "It hurts. Help, help, get it off!"

We tried to get it off. But it wouldn't come off. We pulled and pulled and pulled. I would hold Joe around the waist while Andy pulled on the rattle. It looked like Joe's neck got longer and his head distorted, but still the rattle would not come off. He kept on crying and begging.

Finally, we got him to sit down on the bottom of the playpen, wrap his arms around the wooden bars, and put his chin on the top rail. Andy and I both got on the outside and pulled together. All of a sudden, the rattle came loose with a loud *Pop!* and Andy and I tumbled backwards onto the floor.

When we got to our feet and looked at Joe, he did not look quite right. There in the center of his forehead was a big, round, red, sucked-up place. And we discovered soon that it would not wash off!

I knew what to do. All we needed to do, I thought, was to cover it up with some of Mama's makeup.

When we went to look for the makeup, it was nowhere to be found. So we began to look in all the cabinets in the bathroom. There had to be something there that would work. Suddenly, Andy picked up a large bottle. "Let's try this!" he suggested.

I looked at the familiar bottle. It was what was always used when we had poison ivy or an insect bite: a large, full bottle of pink calamine lotion.

"Stop crying," we told Joe. "We are going to fix you. You are going to be better than new!"

We found cotton balls and, together, finally managed to get the bottle open. Andy gave the directions, and I did the application. We soaked a cotton ball with calamine lotion, and I dabbed it all around over the big red place on Joe's forehead.

It covered it up completely, but now it was pink.

Andy came to the rescue. "If you put it all the way across his forehead," he suggested, "it will look even, and she won't even notice it."

I put the pink lotion carefully across Joe's forehead and down to the corners of his eyebrows. This did not look like it helped. Now, he looked like an old two-tone car.

"Put some more on," was Andy's only suggestion.

I put on more and more. There just never was a good stopping place. In no time, the big bottle was totally empty, and wherever he was not wearing a diaper Joe was a shining, solid pink baby all over. He looked good!

Just at that time, Mama came back from the garden. She had a large bucket of beans that she was going to work on while she sat on the back porch. We came out the door to meet her as she arrived.

"How's the baby?" she asked.

"Fine."

"Did you watch him?"

"Yes."

"Do I need to check on him?"

"*Nooo!*" Andy and I answered in unison this time.

"Oh? I think I better check on him."

When she walked in the kitchen door and saw my smiling, solid pink little brother, she almost shrieked. "He's sick!" Immediately, she grabbed him up in her left arm and put her right hand on his forehead to see if he had a temperature. She left the hand there just long enough that when she removed it, all of the pink stuff came right off on her hand, and there it was, uncovered: the big, sucked-up red place!

I realized in that moment how completely my mother could get mad in a hurry. She totally lost her punctuation. It was going to be one sentence until the end of the day: "What in the world have you done to my baby I can't take my eyes off of you for ten minutes what have you done to him you can't be trusted farther than I can throw you...." All I could think was that this story was going to have a very bad ending.

Then the unbelievable happened. I could not believe what I heard. She was still going: "I am as mad as a wet hen look at me when I am talking to you...."

Then came these magic words: "You two boys you two boys

you two boys never never never get to watch him again!"

We did it! We got fired from watching the baby. And from then on, no matter what I was doing, I never again had to watch the baby.

Chapter 2

TOO MUCH HAIR

B ack when I was on the way to being born, my mother had a terrible, terrible, terrible time getting me here. When I finally arrived, I was a very banged-up, squashed, and bruised little baby.

Mama and I stayed in the hospital for a pretty long time, so I am told. It was 1944, and everyone stayed in the hospital for a long time back then. Finally, someone decided it was time for us to go home, so we did.

As usually happens, people began to come by to visit Mama and to admire the new baby. I use the word *admire* because that is what people normally do when judging new babies, "Oh, how cute," being the usual verdict.

In this case, it was different. The visitors would cheer Mama, who had indeed endured a very difficult childbirth, then they would look cautiously at me. The most often reported response was, "Don't worry, he'll get better!" I was the family's ugly baby.

Looking back later, I realized that being ugly does not hurt you if you don't know it. So I got along just fine for nearly three years. Then a national disaster occurred right in our own family: I got a little brother!

For nearly three years, I had never given one single thought to having a need for a little brother. It had never once occurred to me to ask for one. My parents got him anyway.

My little brother, Joe, was a Cesarean baby, and as soon as he arrived, everyone thought he was beautiful! Visitors to see the new baby kept coming, and I had to listen to all the comments: "Isn't he beautiful?" "Isn't he a darling?" "He's precious!" "His head's not squashed like that other one was!" "*Look* at that hair!"

This was the situation: my mother and I both had what Mother called "little mouse hair." It was thin and fine and nondescript brown. But our daddy had thick, wavy, curly, almost-black hair. My new brother, Joe, had gotten his hair from Daddy.

Mama loved his hair. She would roll it around in her fingers with constant verbal admiration: "Oh, it is so beautiful, it is so beautiful. I wish I had hair like that!" Her often-used compound description of Joe's hair was, "Naturally curly, wasted on a boy."

Only I knew the real truth. No matter how many times Mama insisted that she wished for hair like Joe's hair, I knew that what she really wanted was not a baby boy with curly hair; what she really wanted was a little girl. I figured this out because I was the first one to notice that she refused to cut Joe's hair.

As he grew, his hair grew with him. It got longer and longer, curlier and curlier. In no time, he and I looked like a little boy and his cute little sister. We would go with Mama on trips to town, and strangers would come up to look into the baby buggy. When they saw Joe, they would beam to Mama, "Oh, what a perfectly darling little girl you have!"

I was totally embarrassed. I would think, almost out loud, *He's not a girl. Look in his diaper. He's not a girl!* It was terrible.

This went on and on. Years actually passed. My little brother,

Joe, got to be five years old, and in his entire life he had never had one single haircut. He looked like either Shirley Temple or a miniature version of a television wrestler. Still, Mama loved his hair.

The summer when he was five years old, one topic of conversation seemed to dominate every family visit. From Grandma and Granddaddy to every aunt and uncle, the same question came: "Will Lucille cut Joe's hair before he starts to school in September?"

Opinion was divided. Daddy said, "We need to cut his hair, Lucille. The children at school will tease him and make fun of him. At home, it doesn't matter because we love him. Besides that, if someone comes to see us, we can hide him in the closet. But at school, the children will call him a girl. Then he will go into the wrong bathroom, and when he comes out, he will not know who he is. We need to cut his hair!"

Mama could almost not reply. Her eyes would fill with tears whenever cutting Joe's hair was mentioned. She would nearly sob and finally stifle it. "I don't think I can do it. It is so beautiful. I don't think I can do it!"

Our daddy had one favorite hobby. It was called "annoying Mama." He had a large variety of ways of practicing this hobby, but this particular summer he invented a new way.

He found, way back in an old drawer in a bedroom, an old-fashioned pair of hair clippers saved from his own childhood. They were the very clippers his own mother had used on his brothers and him when they were small.

The clippers did not plug in. No, they had two handles specially shaped for your thumb and fingers, and they worked smoothly and perfectly once Daddy cleaned and oiled the works.

He would pull out the clippers and chase my brother, crying after him, "I'm going to get you, I'm going to get you. I'm going to snatch you bald headed!"

Joe thought it was great fun. He played his role to the hilt.

He would run and scream at the top of his lungs, "Mama, Mama, save me! Daddy's going to cut off all my hair!" He was laughing all the while.

Mama would be furious. "Stop it, stop it, stop it!" She would rein both of them in. "I give up. I will cut his hair. I will cut it myself the night before he goes to school. But nobody else better touch him!" Since she was looking directly at my father when these words were spoken, I knew they had nothing to do with me.

It was late summer. School had not started. Every day Joe and I spent playing out of doors. Sometimes, we played in the yard. Sometimes, we played in the dirt of the garden. Occasionally, we played in the barn loft down in the cow pasture. Our favorite place, however, was to cross the little creek behind the barn and play in the woods on the other side. Mama never came across the creek, and when we went over there she didn't know what we were doing.

All summer long, we seemed to have company. The week before, our cousins from Florida had been at our house for a week-long visit. We loved it when they came because they always brought us fascinating presents.

One year, they brought us little baby stuffed alligators. Joe loved his. I told him that if he put it in water, it would wake up and come back to life. He put it into the bathtub and filled the tub with water. The little alligator was stuffed with sawdust, and as the stuffing started to absorb water it began to swell. "Look, Joe." I pointed. "See, it's growing!"

We watched as the alligator grew round and tight. Suddenly, it seemed to explode, and the wet sawdust flew all over the bathroom! Mama made me clean it up, and I was forced to give him my alligator. It was worth it, though, just to see him cry.

This year, though, there were no more alligators. No, this year, they brought us wonderful little molded-rubber Disney character hats. We loved the bright hats. Mine was Donald Duck, all yellow with a blue little cap of his own on top. Joe's was Mickey Mouse. Mama told us that wearing hats in the house was not polite and we should wear them when we were playing outside.

So, on this late-summer day, Joe and I were in the woods across the creek playing imaginary games as Donald Duck and Mickey Mouse. All of a sudden, Joe pulled off his Mickey Mouse hat. "Something is wrong with this hat," he announced. "It stinks! And it's making my head all slick and wet."

I laughed. "You're wearing a rubber hat on a hot day in the summer. It's making you sweat."

"I don't sweat," was his answer. "I'm just a little boy. Old men sweat."

"Well, then"—I was careful not to smile while I looked at him—"it must have finally happened. You have too much hair. You are going to have to get a haircut."

Joe looked at me so innocently. "Where do you get one?"

I looked back with equal innocence. "You sit right there under that tree. I will be right back!"

I silently eased in through the back door of the house. Mama was busy in the kitchen; she didn't even know I was there.

One of the things I knew about our house was the contents of every single drawer in every single piece of furniture in the entire house. So I knew exactly where to go to retrieve the little hair clippers from their own hiding place.

With the clippers out of sight in my pocket, I slipped back out the door and headed over to the woods. Joe was patiently waiting. By now, his curly hair had dried and was flopping all around his shoulders.

"Come and get behind this big tree so I can see better."

He followed my orders.

I looked at his long, beautiful hair—the hair that my mother loved. Suddenly, I had two overwhelming thoughts. *If I actually mess with his hair, I am going to be in bad trouble.* Then I thought, almost out loud, *I am going to do it anyway!*

Suddenly, as I studied Joe's head, I had a vision of our grandfather. Our granddaddy Walker had very white hair, but his hair had a peculiar growing habit. His hair only grew right around the edges of his head. On top of his head, he looked like he had been oiled and polished. He was totally to-the-skin bald.

The question seemed to come out of my mouth all on its own: "How would you like to look like Granddaddy?"

Joe smiled. "That would be fine!"

I started to work. First, I mowed a little road from his forehead right back toward the crown of his head. Then I started to widen it out carefully so that I cleared the top but stopped right at the edges. Once in a while, Joe would reach up and rub his little fingers over the part that I had cut. "Wooo! That's fuzzy!" was his report.

"Do you like that?" I checked it out with him.

"Yeah, that's a lot better now!"

Looking at him, I realized that he had been transformed from Shirley Temple to Benjamin Franklin. It was a good job. We ran around in the woods and played like that for the rest of the afternoon. We were getting tired out when Mama called from the back door, "Supper's ready. Come to supper!"

As we started toward the house, I suggested to Joe, "When we go in the house, be sure to keep your hat on."

"But we're not supposed to wear them in the house. Mama said so," he objected.

"New rules. Now we are," I assured him.

When we entered the kitchen, no one was in there. Every afternoon when Daddy got home from work, he went in the living room, turned the radio on, and went to sleep in the big chair.

Mama had gone to wake him up for supper.

Joe and I sat down in our chairs and waited. It was only a moment until Mama came back into the kitchen. The first thing she spotted was Joe wearing his Mickey Mouse hat at the supper table. She shook her head. "You forgot something, sweetheart. You remember that we don't wear hats at the table. I don't even like hats in the house. Now, take off your hat so we can eat."

Joe smiled, nodded his head forward, and removed the hat. His freshly cleaned head was shining directly at Mama. She let out a scream. Then it sounded and felt like she was sucking all of the air out of the kitchen. It was like a long, slow wail. Then all the air went out of her, and she deflated and landed.

As soon as Mama landed, I knew that she was our mother. She did not even begin to talk to my brother. She started talking to me. I thought, *Why are you talking to me? Talk to him! He's the one with the haircut.*

Then she started asking questions. She didn't ask, "What happened to him?" No, the trial was over. Her only question was, "What did you do to him?"

I couldn't think of what to say. Without even having the thought, I heard my voice answering her question: "I guess he got too close to the fence, and a big cow licked his hair off!"

Her face did not look human.

In the middle of all this, Daddy came in the kitchen door from his nap in the living room. When he saw my brother, Joe, he started slapping his knees and laughing his head off.

That is what made Mama mad at him. She turned on him. "Stop laughing. This is not funny!" All of us thought it was funny, and I wondered what was wrong with her sense of humor.

Mama continued, "Stop that laughing this minute. He needs to be punished, not laughed at!"

I was mystified. *Why*, I wondered, *does my brother need to be punished? He didn't do anything.* Then I caught on. She was talking about me.

Daddy looked at me. "Let's go out into the backyard. And you bring a chair from the kitchen."

"Oh, no! He's going to kill me with a chair!"

Once in the backyard, Daddy told me to sit in the chair, sit on my hands, and not move my hands no matter what happened. Then he slowly pulled the clippers out of his pocket, ceremoniously handed them to my brother, and said, "It's your turn now. Do whatever you want to do!"

It took no more than ten minutes for my brother to finish with me. When he got through, my head looked like a science-fiction planet from outer space.

It was on a Friday when all this happened. My brother, Joe, and I both played all day Saturday with our new haircuts. Then, on Sunday morning, we were shocked. Mama announced that we had to go to Sunday school and church looking like we did: five-year-old Benjamin Franklin and a science-fiction planet from the far reaches of space. We were the providers of all the humor that was there that Sunday at the Methodist church.

On Monday afternoon, Daddy finally took us to the barbershop. Herschel Caldwell, our barber, took one look at us and quickly stepped back. "Wow! I've never seen anything like this! What am I supposed to do about it?"

Daddy chuckled his answer: "Skin 'em good, Herschel, skin 'em good!"

And that is why, on the first day of school that year, both Joe and I entered our classrooms totally and completely bald.

For some reason, no one in the family could ever find the hair clippers again . . . and Mama said she knew nothing about it!

Chapter 3

GOLF TEES

From the time of my earliest memory, I loved to go shopping with Mama. After Joe was born, I loved these trips
even more. Mama would call either Aunt Esther or our
old neighbor, Miss Annie, and ask to leave Joe with them for most
of the day. Then she and I would go to town. It was one of the
only times that I reclaimed her entire attention after she had two
of us to deal with.

I loved it when we went to the dime store. Waynesville was
too little to have Woolworth's—no, you had to make a trip to
Asheville for that. We had Eagles, and it was just fine. There was
more there than I could get into.

It was wonderful when we went to Smith's Drug Store for
our lunch. We would sit in a wooden booth and order grilled
cheese sandwiches and a fresh-made orangeade or cherry smash
to drink. Sometimes, we might have an ice-cream cone for our
dessert.

My favorite stores were Parkman's and Joe Howell's hardware
stores. If we went there, there was a lot for me to play with or get

into before she finished her business and found me.

The store that I hated to go into was Hugh Massie's Toggery.

Mr. Massie was one of the main leaders at the Methodist church. He and Mrs. Massie sat near the front on the left, and they never missed a Sunday. Some people in town even called our church "Hugh Massie's church." I knew he was important.

Mr. Massie was not the reason that I did not like the store. No, he was a very kind and friendly man. It was just that he did not plan The Toggery with children's interests in mind. They had nothing in that store but women's clothes. There must have been ten thousand women's dresses, each one of them different from all the others. They were all on hangers in what looked like long wooden closets with no doors on them. Some of the long, open closets were along the walls, and others were in rows out in the floor.

There was a Shoe Department and a Hat Department and a Belt Department and an Underwear Department and a Coat Department. Not a single one of these had one single thing that a little boy found to be of any interest at all.

Mama loved to go into The Toggery. She was almost never planning to buy anything. She just wanted to go in there and look. She also wanted to talk incessantly with the ladies that worked there about everything and everyone under the sun. She would look for hours through the racks of dresses, gradually choosing a few to take back into one of the dressing rooms to try on. I knew she was not buying anything on any of these miserable days. She would try each one on, then come out to get the opinion of one of the ladies who was in charge of the sales. Every time, the dress that she tried seemed to have something wrong about it, so there was an excuse to put it back and try ten more.

Mr. Massie had nothing at all to do with any of this. He mostly stayed up in an office that was above the front windows of the store. You could look up and see him there, looking down on his Toggery world.

The more Mama loved to go to The Toggery, the more I hated it. I did learn, however, that if she was totally out of sight in the dressing room for a safe period of time, I could climb over into the bottom of one of the open closets where all the dresses were hanging and crawl up and down under them. I could even get behind the dresses and move up and down the length of the whole parade of them, sometimes separating two of them so I could look out to see who and what happened to be in that part of the store.

There were even times when I deliberately stood right behind dresses that were being looked through by some old lady. The old lady would separate the dresses to look at the front of one, and there I was, like a ghost in the back of the rack, silently startling the shopper. Most of the ones to whom that happened quickly picked up their pocketbooks and left the store.

One day, Mama had dragged me to The Toggery for a semester of shopping. I was by now about five or six years old. She had made several trips into the dressing room already and was headed back for an additional term. By now, I had crawled over into the bottom of one of the open closets that seemed to be filled with a long row of skirts. This gave me more room to explore than did the dresses.

As I was crawling along under the skirts, hoping to come upon some old lady to startle, I felt, then saw, an unusual skirt. The first, to me, odd thing about it was that it was made out of the same material I had only before seen used to make blue jeans. I had no idea that other clothes could be made of denim. I stood up to study this strange piece of apparel.

The skirt was straight, about knee length, and at the top it had an unusual belt that was partly made into the top edge of the skirt. The belt was of a woven material, and it went in and out of the wide top hem of the skirt as it went around it.

Then I saw the most interesting thing of all. On either side of the front of the skirt, at two of the places where the belt disappeared into the hem, there were three little leather loops that had three red golf tees stuck in them—three on each side of the skirt, right where you could reach them if you were playing golf. I knew that this was a skirt for women who played golf and that the tees were a wonderful and appropriate decoration.

I reached out and touched the golf tees. An amazing thing then happened. Without my even thinking about it, the six golf tees, three from each side, came right out in my hands and ended up in the pocket of my pants. I did not have to think about or decide to do this. My own independent hands themselves took care of it on their own.

Just at that moment, Mama was finished in the dressing room. She returned all of the dresses she had been trying on and began to call for me. I eased out of the bottom of the skirt rack and fetched up for her.

Mama told the store ladies she would be back later, and we headed out the door and went home. Since I was about six years old, I forgot all about the golf tees in no more than five minutes.

We went by Aunt Esther's house to get my brother, Joe, where Mama had left him while we went shopping. This involved a good thirty-minute visit. Aunt Esther could not tell anyone her name in less than twenty minutes to start with.

Back in the car, there was a stop at Ralph's Cash Grocery on the way home. By the time we arrived home at Plott Creek, the golf tees were deeply gone from any usable memory. I played in the floor with Joe, Mama cooked supper, Daddy came home, we ate supper, and it was time to go to bed.

"When you get your pajamas on," Mama instructed, "throw

your dirty clothes out the door of your bedroom. I am going to start a load of wash before we go to bed." And it was done.

Mama had a very bad habit when it came to washing children's clothes. Instead of minding her own business and simply throwing things into the washing machine, she insisted on emptying the pockets of everything we wore before washing anything.

I was almost asleep when the door of the bedroom abruptly opened.

"Where did you get these?" she asked without explaining what she was talking about.

I opened and rubbed my sleep eyes and then saw, there in her open palm, six red golf tees.

"Where did I get what?" I asked dumbly.

"Don't you start acting like that. You can see what I am talking about. Where did you get these golf tees?"

"I can't remember right now. I was asleep."

Mama did not stop. In no time, I was out of bed and sitting at the kitchen table. The six red golf tees were arrayed on the kitchen table like witnesses for the prosecution. I was on trial.

It was a Thursday night. I know that now because Daddy was not at home. That meant it had to be Thursday night, since Thursday night was Lion's Club night and the only regular night he was ever out for supper during the week. So there was no hope of rescue.

Eventually, the truth came out. I whimpered and wailed and finally told Mama that I had taken the golf tees out of the loops on the skirt at The Toggery. She was red-faced and furious. What was worst of all was my deep sense of her disappointment in me. I could not stop crying.

Mama told me that the next day we were going to go back to town. We were going to take the golf tees with us. We were going to go straight to The Toggery. I was then going to go upstairs to Mr. Hugh Massie's office and tell Mr. Massie what I had done. After I confessed, I was going to beg for forgiveness and promise Mr. Massie that I would never in my life do anything like that again. Mama and I were both crying by now.

She sent me back to bed. I could not for anything in the world manage to fall asleep. Now, I had Mr. Massie to worry about. The next day played itself out visually in my mind over and over again in slightly different ways. Most of the differences were simple differences in the ways Mr. Massie would probably execute me after the confession was made. I cried myself to the edge of dehydration and, exhausted, fell asleep.

By morning, my mind had, all on its own, come up with an idea. I waited patiently until after Daddy had left for work before approaching Mama. She was sitting at the kitchen table, nursing a cup of coffee. Her face did not look good.

"Mama." I softly approached her. "I have an idea I want to talk about with you. Is this a good time . . . before we go to town?"

"What is it?" She sounded very tired. "I could use almost any kind of good idea. So, what is it?"

"Well, I was just thinking. If the golf tees got put back into the belt of the skirt, it would be just like nothing had ever happened. So why don't we just go up there to The Toggery, and, while you try on a dress, I will put the golf tees back where they came from, and it will be like we skipped over yesterday and it never did happen. Nobody really wants to talk about golf tees. That's my idea."

She almost smiled. "That's a wonderful idea. Let's get ready and go do that. You can put them back, and we don't need to ever say anything else ever again."

We started out. The Toggery was fairly busy in the middle of the morning on a Friday when we got there. Mama, without even looking at the size or anything else about them, grabbed three dresses from the first long, open closet and headed to the dressing room to try them on.

One of the salesladies trailed her. "Lucille, I think you tried that yellow dress on yesterday."

"I know I did." Mama did not even look at the dress. "I'm not sure I gave it a good chance, so I'm going to try it again. I don't need any help with it."

By then, I was under the skirts. In no time, the denim skirt was located. In less time than you can imagine, the six red golf tees were at home back in the little loops on the belt of the skirt.

I walked back to the dressing room and softly knocked on the door.

"I said I didn't need any help." Mama thought the saleslady was knocking.

"I know, Mama." I spoke through the door quietly. "And now I don't need any more help either."

Out the door she came, and we went home.

Mama never spoke to me again about what happened on those two days. But that night, I did overhear an interesting conversation she had with my daddy. I realized at the outset that they must have talked the night before, as he asked her for a report on the trip to The Toggery.

Mama started, "It turned out better than I thought. He got a good idea. He offered to put the tees back where he got them if we would just go up there quietly and not bother anybody. We did it, and now it is all over."

"I thought you had a different plan. I thought you were going to make him confess to Hugh," Daddy wondered.

"Oh, Joe." Mama's voice sounded so strained. "I got too mad

when I made that threat. I worried myself to death over it. You see, I realized that if he actually did that, I would be the one to be embarrassed."

"I don't understand," Daddy still wondered.

"Let me tell you." Mama was sounding more relieved now. "If he had done what I first had in mind, then Mr. Hugh Massie would have known that I raised my child to be a thief. I would have been so embarrassed that I might not be able to look at him in church again, let alone go back in The Toggery. That idea saved me. Now, the damage is repaired, and Mr. Massie still knows that I am a good mother after all. It is over."

That night, I slept easily. There was now nothing about which to worry. But I did wonder whether I would ever come to understand the deep and weird reasoning of some adults.

Chapter 4

GO LOOK IT UP!

When I was growing up, there were a lot of things that had not been invented. One of those things was called "self-esteem." Since self-esteem had not been invented, it did not need to be taken care of. It was a different world.

When we got in trouble, no one was put in "timeout." Timeout would simply have been a nice, quiet opportunity to think up more troublesome stuff to do. There was no such thing as "grounded." No, here is the way it went: if you got into trouble at home, you got a flat-out, uncaged, free-range whipping.

But at school, it was different. If you got into trouble at school, you got a paddling. The difference was legal. If you got spanked with a paddle, the teacher could later stand up in court and truthfully swear, "I did not touch him!" Every teacher I ever had in school taught with a paddle. It was standard equipment.

In the first grade, Mrs. Annie Ledbetter used a red Fli-Back paddle. The Fli-Back paddles were manufactured for the teaching industry by the Fli-Back Toy Company in High Point, North

Carolina, and they came disguised as toys. The new paddles arrived as gifts on birthdays and Christmas. They were wooden paddles with a long rubber band stapled right in the center. On the other end of the rubber band, there was a small red rubber ball. The deception was that if you practiced long enough at trying to hit the rubber ball with the paddle, eventually you would be able to intercept the ball when the rubber band returned it faster than you had hit it, and again knock it with the paddle before it hit you square in the eye.

That first-grade year, it was William Birchfield who got one of these Fli-Back paddles on his birthday. William brought it to school. We could see it sticking out of his back pocket. While Mrs. Ledbetter was not looking, William pulled out the paddle and was practicing, *Whackety, whackety, whackety* . . . Mrs. Ledbetter recognized the sound, turned around, and, before William could take a quick breath, lifted the red paddle from his hand, popped the rubber band off of it, and recycled it on the spot! William yelped as the paddle found Mrs. Ledbetter's target on his first-grade rear end.

For the rest of that year, and for the rest of her teaching career, the red paddle dozed on the corner of her desk, ready to sit up and go into action whenever it heard the right tone in her voice.

Even in the first grade, however, I soon discovered that most of us did not have much to worry about. It seemed that in every class of little kids, there was installed in the room two or three designated "paddle-ees," whose role in life was to get paddled for the rest of us. It was the reason they had been placed on the face of the earth.

In Mrs. Ledbetter's class, which was basically the *A*'s through the *Gr*'s (Charlotte Abernethy through Lady Ruth Green), the designated paddling recipients were Tommy Conard, his cousin,

Aldean (they were already genetically related), and a tall, faded-looking boy named Lynn Fowle.

Lynn Fowle was the youngest of seven brothers. Every year, year after year, all seven of the Fowle brothers started the year at Hazelwood School, even though there were only six grades. As the year progressed, the Fowle boys, one at a time and every few weeks, disappeared from school. Gradually, we heard the whispered tales: they were being gradually transported to a mythical land known as "the Stonewall Jackson Training School." It was a faraway place where evil boys would be gathered from all over North Carolina. There, they were all joined together so that they could exchange evil information with one another and each one be a lot worse when returning home than he had ever been to start with.

Every day of the week, Mrs. Ledbetter paddled one of these three boys. On Monday, for example, she paddled Tommy. On Tuesday, it was Aldean. On Wednesday, it was Lynn. On Thursday, back to Aldean. On Friday, she paddled all three of them. She knew that she was going to have to miss paddling them for two days over the weekend, and that they all three needed it anyway. The next week, she would start the paddlings in a different order for fairness.

Finally, we finished the first grade, and all of the A's through the Gr's moved up to Old (that was her first name) Miss Lois Harrell's class.

Old Miss Lois Harrell was profoundly old. She once told us that she had been teaching second grade for one hundred and eighty-three years, and that was after she had taught in all the other grades to find out for sure where she really belonged.

Old Miss Lois Harrell was so ancient that she existed on the outer fringes of total dehydration. The only thing that kept her on the face of the earth was a giant bottle of Jergens Lotion that she rubbed into herself all the time to try to keep herself puffed up so that the wind would not simply blow her away.

Old Miss Lois Harrell had an electric paddle!

The electric paddle had been invented by her boyfriend, Harry. In a previous eon, Harry had been slated to marry Old Miss Lois Harrell. But before the wedding time came, the world war came along, and Harry was sent off to fight the Germans. In a short time, he discovered that fighting the Germans was a better prospect than getting married to Old Miss Lois Harrell. So Harry just kept signing up to stay in the army.

After two and a half wars, he finally came home. Now, it was too late to make any point at all by getting married. So he simply eroded into being Old Miss Lois Harrell's boyfriend for life.

Every afternoon, he came over to her house and stayed through suppertime, after which he went home to his own house. But in the middle of all this, he invented the electric paddle.

Years later, I thought back and figured out how he had done it. Harry had taken a board and cut it out into the shape of an elongated paddle. He had then painted it red, except that on one side there was a sort of explosive logo like that which later popped up on television if you were watching *Batman*. Near the end of the handle, Harry had drilled a hole into the wood. Deep into this hole, he had glued one end of an electric wire, on the other end of which was a big plug. Now, the electric paddle was complete.

It lay on top of Old Miss Lois Harrell's desk, tail curled like a sleeping snake, waiting to be called into service.

When she got all wound up, Old Miss Lois Harrell would pick up the paddle. Its long electric tail would unroll and dangle to the floor. Then she would proclaim, "I am going to do you a favor today, boys and girls. I am going to use the paddle by hand.

But you listen to me! If you keep on acting like this, I am going to be forced to plug it in! I cannot even begin to tell you what happens when I plug it in. It might get out of control and use itself on every one of you!"

We were paralyzed with fear, especially after the fifth- and sixth-graders told us about how she had actually plugged it in when they were back in the second grade. They told us that a little boy totally melted through the floor of the classroom—so totally, in fact, that they could not remember his name and his own family could not remember that they had ever had him. It was terrifying.

The same three victims—Aldean, Tommy, and Lynn—were in Old Miss Lois Harrell's room. Just like in the first grade, one or more of them got the paddle almost every day. It was routine.

One afternoon after lunch, Old Miss Lois decided that it was time to give a dose to Tommy. She had him bent over a desk and was warming up her paddling arm. When she started paddling, Old Miss Lois did not take into account that she had just been rubbing a whole gob of Jergens Lotion into her hands and the lotion had not yet soaked in.

Tommy was hanging on to the desk. The paddle was singing its song. About the time it got up to seventy-eight RPMs, the paddle slipped out of Old Miss Lois Harrell's hand and flew in an arc through the air, dragging its electric tail behind it. The paddle struck the upper pane of the big, tall schoolhouse window, the glass shattered into hundreds of pieces, and we watched the paddle go out the window and fall toward the sidewalk below.

Just as the window shattered, Mr. Buck Bowles, the superintendent, was coming up the walk to visit Mr. Leatherwood, our principal. That may be what changed the course of the afternoon.

In only a moment, Mr. Leatherwood and Mr. Bowles both

arrived at our classroom door. We students had already taken the initiative and were, on our own, cleaning up the broken glass, as Old Miss Lois seemed to be paralyzed by the turn of events. Suddenly, Miss Lois left the room with Mr. Leatherwood and Mr. Bowles, and we had an instant substitute: Haskel Davis, our janitor.

It was a great afternoon. Haskel got a stepladder and let us help him cut cardboard and fill in the broken window. Then he spent the last hour of the day telling us stories about fire, blood, and throw-up!

We went home.

The next morning when we got to school, there was a new pane of glass in the window. As soon as the morning roll was called and lunch money was taken up, we lined up to go to the auditorium for an unannounced all-school assembly. When we got there, we saw that both Mr. Leatherwood and Mr. Bowles were up on the stage. It was going to be a long and serious meeting.

Mr. Bowles did the talking. "Boys and girls," he started. (Mr. Bowles had a habit of rattling the change in his pocket while he talked. It was like the bell on the cat, and we were the mice.) "Yesterday afternoon after school, we had a special teacher workshop on discipline," he went on. "Things are changing here at Hazelwood Elementary School. We decided yesterday that there will be no more paddling in school."

About three boys out of every thirty students applauded.

"Now, listen to me." He was not finished. "I did not say that there would be no punishment. No, because many of you are still evil. It is just going to be different. There is a new kind of punishment that has been invented. They are doing it at schools all over the country, and we are going to try it here at Hazelwood Elementary School. It is called 'getting suspended.'"

Mr. Bowles went on to explain everything in great detail. There would be two levels of "getting suspended." First, there was the misdemeanor level. He read off a list of minor offenses and told us that any of these would result in "getting suspended in school." We would be put in a special room with all the other students who were being suspended in school, and we would all be suspended in there together with a teacher watching us.

Then there was the felony level. This was a serious list. It included things like fighting on the school bus (especially fighting with the driver), stealing lunch money, changing grades on your report card (but only if you made them better), and, worst of all, calling a teacher the same thing you had already heard your parents call them. If you did any of these things, you would be suspended out of school on your own! That was it.

With this last pronouncement, the assembly was over, and we marched out of the auditorium and back to our second-grade class.

Once we were back in the room and settled down, Old Miss Lois Harrell looked us over and asked, "So, boys and girls, did you all understand what Mr. Bowles told us?"

"Yes!" It was Tommy who answered for the class. "No more paddling!"

"That's right, Tommy," she intoned. "But there is to be punishment. From now on, you are going to get suspended instead of paddled. Is that clear? Do any of you have any questions at all about this? I want it to be clear."

Near the back of the room, a little boy named Eddie Curtis raised his hand. Every year, Eddie would be seated near the back of the room. I remember often seeing his eyes closed for long periods of time in the school day.

"Eddie"—she saw his raised hand—"do you have a question?"

"Yes, ma'am. I heard everything Mr. Bowles said, but he just didn't make it clear to me. There were a lot of big words. Just what does *suspended* mean, anyway?"

The entire class wondered the same thing Eddie did. Mr. Bowles had worn that word out for most of a good hour and had not one time actually told us what the word itself meant.

Being a good second-grade teacher, Old Miss Lois Harrell did not answer the question. No, we already knew what she was going to say: "Go look it up!"

Every one of us hated that phrase, "Go look it up." Whenever you did not know what a word meant, you heard, "Go look it up." Whenever you did not know how to spell a word, you heard, "Go look it up." How were you supposed to look a word up if you did not know how to spell it to begin with?

I remembered a day when I spent what seemed like hours flipping back and forth between *c* and *k* trying to find katsup/cetchup/catsup/ketchup or whatever was in the dictionary. It was torture.

We all watched as little Eddie trudged over to the dictionary. It was a gigantic and heavy *New Century Dictionary*, a dark red color. Old Miss Lois Harrell had acquired it, one section at a time, over a year of shopping at the A&P store. Now, it was finished and bolted together for all of us to use.

Eddie opened the big book and started turning toward *s*. Soon, he was to the *su*'s.

Suddenly, Eddie spotted the word. His back arched, his eyes rolled back in his head, and he wailed, "*Nooo!* Jesus, Joseph, and Mary, they are going to *hang* us! If you are just a little bit bad, they are going to put you in a room with all the children who are a little bit bad and hang us all together with a teacher watching. If you are really bad, they are going to drag you out of school and hang you all by yourself without even having anyone to watch. *Nooo!*"

The entire class fell apart.

Two days later in the Waynesville *Mountaineer*, the following headline appeared near the bottom of the third page: "Twenty-eight second-graders petition school board to re-establish paddling as their preferred form of punishment."

And it was done.

Chapter 5

LITTLE CRITTERS

From the time I was born until after Joe was born, I never once spent the night away from home. This meant that I had never had a night not spent in the same house with my mama. I thought, of course, that this was normal, not knowing that many other children had unwatched adventures with no mother present.

After Joe came along, however, Mama was very tired. It was not long until I was regularly being invited to spend a night, or more, at my grandmother's house. This was the delight of my early life. Grandma Walker thought that I was infinitely cute and extremely smart. I loved time at her house.

Grandma and Granddaddy Walker lived about a dozen miles out of town in the Fines Creek community, just over Rush Fork Gap from Crabtree. It was the farm on which Mama had grown up, a place she did not remember fondly but where I loved adventure and play.

After a dozen miles in the car on the paved road, we would turn off and stop at a big gate. My job was to get out and open the gate, hold it until the car went through, then swing it closed. It was another long mile down the farm road to the house. Since Granddaddy did not drive, the road condition was no concern to him. He actually preferred it washed out, to prevent accidental company from curiously wandering down the road.

The house was old and made of logs, but they were now covered with boards and did not show. There was no electricity or running water in the house. Cooking was on a wood stove, light was by candles and lanterns, and water was carried in from the spring a few steps out the kitchen door in the back of the house.

With no indoor plumbing, there was no bathroom in the house. Instead, there was an outhouse a few yards above the house on the way to the barn. It was a large outhouse with two seats side by side. In a family as large as Mama's was when she was a child, shyness was not part of the family formula.

If you needed an actual bath, it came in a tin tub on the back porch of the house, but this did not happen often if you were a child.

One of the finest things about the trips to Grandma's was that, in the early years, Joe did not go with me. No, he was a baby. The reason I was going to begin with was to give Mama time with him without my being there. My interpretation was that my grandparents wanted only me, and the idea was for me to get all of their attention without having to share a thing.

There was one actual bedroom downstairs in the house. It was the room where my grandparents slept. There was also a room called "the front room" that served various purposes, from visiting with company to classing tobacco to occasional bedroom. The other permanent sleeping space was one big, long room that made up the entire second story of the house. My mother and her six sisters had grown up in that room, and it was filled with a varying number of beds at different times.

There was only one ongoing problem with spending time at Grandma's house: it was called my uncle Sonny. He was my mother's baby brother, and he was only a few years older than I was. He was like a big brother I neither needed nor asked for. He seemed to think that I was his personal science experiment. He worked at always continuing to find new ways to trick and scare me. I did not then realize that he was simply making up for having come into a world already occupied by six sisters and an older brother.

My uncle Sonny now occupied the second-floor bedroom in the log house. It was his domain, and I did not at all like going up there. It was a spooky place to me.

Whenever I visited overnight at Grandma's house, I slept in the same room with Grandma and Granddaddy. When I was three and four years old, I slept between the two of them, right there in the deep middle of the feather bed. It was always warm, even in the coldest weather.

When I got to be a little bit older, I still slept in their bedroom. Now, I was too big to share the feather bed, so Grandma made me a little pallet on the floor by folding several of her homemade quilts and placing them on top of one another until I had a fairly comfortable and private bed of my own.

I got to be eight years old the summer after the second grade in school. Joe was five, and this would be his last summer at home before going to church-basement kindergarten. Mama wanted time with him.

It was a total surprise one day when Mama announced to me, "Your grandmother has invited you to come and spend a week with her. A whole week! You should really like that. Get your clothes ready, because we are going today!"

I knew nothing of what might have really gone on in securing this invitation. I was simply delighted at the prospect of the coming week: no brother, no father, no mother for me!

With some extra clothes, pajamas, and my toothbrush packed in a brown paper grocery bag, I climbed into the car with the rest of the family. Everyone was going on the little trip to deliver me to Grandma. The only thing I could think of on the way was how long the twelve-mile trip seemed to be before we got there.

The whole family came in and visited for a few minutes. After we caught up on all the news of the family we had somehow missed, it was time for the others to go and leave me to my own devices. I acted like I would miss everyone, and they were gone.

For the rest of the afternoon, I worked with Grandma in her garden. My job was to pull weeds and carry rocks to the edge of the garden. No matter how many years and how many generations of people carried rocks, they never ran out. The rocks seemed to multiply in the bare garden in the wintertime.

Late in the afternoon, we returned to the house. I stayed in the kitchen and watched Grandma as she cooked supper, smelling and tasting along the way. When all was ready, she called Granddaddy and Uncle Sonny. They came in from the barn and washed up on the back porch, and we all gathered at the table.

It was a vegetable supper, all from the garden, with a little bit of leftover sausage from breakfast added in. We were all happily eating and talking at the table when, out of nowhere, Grandma made an announcement to me: "You are now eight years old! My, my, that is old. And you are going to be here with us for a whole week. That will be fun.

"But there is one thing: a week is too long for you to sleep on the floor in our room. You are old enough now that you can go upstairs and share the room with Sonny. There are plenty of beds up there, and the two of you always get along just fine."

Oh, no! I thought to myself. *That is the worst idea in the world. If I am captured up there all night, no telling what will happen to me.* This was not to be a happy time, but Grandma was the law and there was no questioning her about this.

I ate as slowly as possible, trying to put off the inevitable night to come. Finally, there was no way left to stall. It was time to get up from the table and get ready to go to bed.

It was dark by now, and Uncle Sonny had a little old lamp that we were to carry up the stairs so we could see our way to bed. Since there was no electricity anywhere on the farm, there was no light at all coming in any windows from outside. It really was totally pitch-dark.

I gathered my little bag of belongings. First, I went out on the back porch and brushed my teeth, using some water from the drinking-water bucket out there. Then it was time to go.

Sonny led as we climbed the steep stairs. The entire world that I could see was the world illuminated by the lamp he was carrying. The light of the lamp itself made everything outside its circle exceptionally dark. We got to the top of the stairs, and he held up the lamp so you could see most of the long room. There was indeed a collection of several feather beds jammed into the space up there.

He pointed to the bed closest to the top of the stairs. "This is my bed. You can sleep in any bed you want. Just pick one. They are all just about alike anyway."

I looked at the long room and the multiple beds and made my decision. I found my way by the light of the lamp and picked the bed that was the farthest from his bed. It was the bed that was against the wall at the far end of the room. Before he blew out the light, I put on my pajamas and crawled down into the deep covers of the chosen feather bed.

The lamp was out. It was so dark that there was no visual difference between open and closed eyes. I closed them tightly anyway and curled into a tight ball to work on falling asleep.

Sleep had nearly overtaken me when I heard a strange sound. It was coming from the other side of the wall right beside the bed where I was trying to sleep.

The sound got louder. It went, *Skreeek, skreeek, skreeek!* over and over again. What could be making this sound on the outside wall of the house on the second story above the ground?

Before I could get up my courage to ask the question, Uncle Sonny said, "Listen! Do you hear that? They're coming!"

"What's coming?" I almost wailed.

"Those little critters!" was the quick answer.

"What little critters?"

"The ones that live up in the woods."

I couldn't stand this. "What do they look like?"

"They are not very big. Five or six of them could get under your bed. They are hairy and scaly all over, and they have big claws. That's the sound you hear. They are climbing up the outside of the wall. They have huge eyes that glow in the dark and rows and rows of long, sharp teeth."

"What are they going to do?" I was nearly crying now.

"They are looking for a little hole."

"What kind of a little hole?"

He sounded like he was about to chuckle. "A little hole that comes out under your bed!"

It was terrible! I buried myself as deeply under the covers as it was possible to get. I tried to lie as flat as I could, so that it would not look like anyone was in the feather bed. I was terrified to even wiggle my little finger.

Was it possible to sleep like this? Would they give up and

go away soon? Would I be dead or alive in the morning? It never entered my mind that it was a strange thing that Uncle Sonny seemed not to be afraid of the little critters.

As time passed, I realized that I needed to go to the bathroom. Since the actual bathroom was the outdoor outhouse, I knew that there would be an emergency bucket somewhere under the bed. There was no way to get to the bucket, since the screeching noise had stopped and I was certain that the little critters were now hiding silently under my bed. I would simply have to hold it. I might explode in the night, but this would be better than being eaten bite by bite by little hairy things that would disappear back into the woods and leave no sign of me at all.

I did indeed hold it all night. By morning, it was misery beyond description. Uncle Sonny seemed to be happily and soundly still asleep. As soon as I could hear my grandma up and moving downstairs in the kitchen, I leapt out of bed, ran down the stairs, tore out the door to the outhouse, and thought I might actually fill it up.

When I got back to the house, there was no escaping the obvious questions from her: "What in the world were you doing? Is something wrong with you?"

There was no choice but to answer the questions. I told her all about the terrible little creatures and the night of misery that I had endured.

She laughed. Then she shook her head and said, "You are going to have to learn to ignore Sonny, that's all there is to it. Now, come on with me."

She led me around to the backside of the house just below the end where I had tried to sleep the night before.

There near the back of the house stood a large sugar maple tree. It had a broad-crowned top and long limbs, some of which actually touched the walls of the house. As she pointed up at the tree, a gust of wind rounded the house and the biggest of the long limbs rubbed along the upper wall. *Skreeek, skreeek.* The sound was unmistakable.

"Is that what scared you?" The question was simple.

"I guess it was." I hung my head as I answered. I had been scared silly by a maple tree. The realization made me feel like the dumbest child in the world.

After that, I slept just fine and even laughed with Uncle Sonny when we heard the same sound coming back night after night. "They're coming!" I would call out to him, and he would laugh.

At the end of the week, I was picked up by the whole family and went back home. Of course, there were Mama's questions, every one of which was another version of the same thing: "What did you do at your grandma's house all week?" I told her everything I could think of telling, but I left out one thing: I could not bring myself to admit that I had stayed up all night and nearly wet the bed because I had been scared by a tree limb. It was just too embarrassing.

It was a few days later when I was playing with Joe that I had a wonderful realization: I had a little brother. He was a usable little brother, and the time would come when he would get to come with me to stay at Grandma's house, and I would be totally ready for him.

I did not have long to wait. The very next summer, we were visiting at Grandma and Granddaddy's house when Uncle Sonny happened to be away from home. We were getting ready to go home when Grandma asked a question. It was directed to me. "We are here at home by ourselves this week. Would you like to stay and spend the night with us? You haven't been here to stay for a little while."

Before I could answer, Joe piped up, "Can I stay, too? He gets to stay, and I never get to stay! Can I stay, too?"

Before Mama could answer, I jumped in: "Let him stay! He is a big boy now. Let him stay, and I will take care of him!"

And the plan was made. Mama and Daddy left the two of us on a Friday afternoon with the promise that they would come to get us on Sunday. We didn't have any clean clothes with us, but Mama declared that we would be fine for only two days, and we could sleep in our underwear.

Joe and I played all around Grandma's house for the rest of the afternoon. Then she called us to the kitchen for supper. Granddaddy was also there, of course, but he did not have a lot to say to children. At the table, I brought up the sleeping arrangement. It was confirmed by Grandma that I would be in charge of Joe and that the two of us would share the upstairs sleeping room of the house.

Grandma now had a little silver flashlight to give to us to find our way to bed. I lingered at the table to be sure it was good and dark before we headed up the stairs. It would be better that way.

As soon as Joe and I started up the stairs, I knew that this was going to be worth it. He did not even want to go up there. "Why can't I sleep downstairs with Grandma and Granddaddy?" he objected.

"Because"—I had already thought through this—"you are a big boy. Big boys sleep upstairs. Come on. I am going to take good care of you!"

His eyes got bigger and bigger every time we climbed another step.

We got to the top, and I shined the flashlight all around the long room so he could see all that was up there.

"Are we going to sleep together?" he asked, hoping.

"No! You are a big boy! You don't need anyone to sleep with you. You will be fine. Remember, you were the one who wanted to stay in the first place."

He whimpered agreement.

"Here is the plan. This bed right here, near the steps, is my bed. This is where I sleep because I am in charge, and I can watch the steps in case anything goes wrong. Now, for you, the best bed in the whole house is that bed back there by the back wall. I don't think many people ever go back there and sleep in it. It is fresh and good. You will like it back there."

Joe was so scared to go to the back of the room that I had to take him back there with the flashlight and hold it for him to get his clothes off and get into bed. Then I told him good night and made my way back to the bed at the other end of the room. Now, it was time to stay awake and wait for the wind to blow. It did not take long.

Gradually, the wind came slipping around the corner of the house. It got stronger and bolder. Then it happened: *Skreeek, skreeek, skreeek!*

"What's that?" Joe wailed.

"What's what?" I replied innocently. "I didn't hear anything."

"That little screeching noise. It sounds like something is right through the wall!" He was scared.

"Oh! They must be coming!" This was going to be good.

"What?"

"The little critters!" I was trying not to sound tickled.

"What little critters?"

I had had a full year to think about this, so I was ready to make it really good. "Little critters who live out in the woods. They are scaly and hairy at the same time. They are not very big. Five or six of them could fit under your bed. You hear them climbing up the wall outside because they have sharp claws instead of fingernails."

Joe was listening to every word. "What are they going to do?"

"I think they are looking for a little hole in the wall."

"What for?"

Suddenly, I got a new idea! "They are hungry."

"What do they eat?"

"I've heard that they like tender meat. I've heard that they eat the meat off of your legs and then suck all the blood out of you while you are trying to run away on the bare bones!" Even I knew that this was over the edge.

For the next twenty minutes or so, the only sound I could hear was my little brother sobbing and wailing. The only reason that Grandma could not hear him was that his head was deeply buried away under the covers of the bed, as he tried to be so far out of sight that the little critters could not eat him.

Finally, he cried until no more sound would come out. It got so quiet that I thought he might have actually fallen asleep. Then I heard another distinct sound. It was the *Drip, drip, drip, drip* sound of water.

Then I realized what was happening. He could not hold it as long as I could, and he had so totally wet the bed that it had gone through the feather mattress and was now flooding down into the floor. I did not sleep much after that. I knew that there would be payment time in the morning.

When morning came, there was nothing in the world that could have stopped the story he told Grandma. She listened as I emerged as the main character in Joe's story of the long night before.

When he was all finished, she looked at me and called me the same thing Mama called me when she was mad. "Well, mister, you have a few things to do."

There were three.

I had to take my brother around to the back of the house and show him the big maple tree and promise him that there were no little critters back there or anywhere at all in the woods.

Then I had to give him my dry clothes. Since we had stayed without preparation, I had to spend two days with no underwear until Mama came back to get us on Sunday. It was not pleasant.

I also had to clean up the floor under the bed and pull off all the covers. Grandma helped me pull the feather mattress out into the sunshine for it to dry. It dried, but when we put it back and I had to make up the bed, it still had a memorable smell.

Once I got that done, I thought everything was over. I was wrong. We had another night to spend before returning home on the next day. When it came to be time for bed, Grandma walked the two of us upstairs. When we got there, her new announcement came: "Joe, I want you to sleep here in the bed at the top of the stairs. That way, you can call me if you have any trouble."

Then she looked at me. "And you, mister, since you think that the bed at the end of the room is the best bed, I think you should sleep back there."

"It stinks!" The words came out before I even thought about what I was saying.

"Good! So does what you did. You can sleep back there, and maybe the smell will help you remember how you treated your brother, and you will not do that again."

Chapter 6

BOYS ARE SMARTER?

After that first time Joe and I stayed together at Grandma's house, there was no problem in our being there together ever again. I had learned good lessons about what "take care of" actually meant, and Mama and Grandma knew that I could now forever be trusted with him. There were hardly any new trips there alone. From that time on, I was stuck with my brother.

The following summer, when I was nine and he was approaching seven, a new opportunity came. Mother again made the announcement: "Boys, get your stuff together. Your grandmother and granddaddy want both of you to come for a week. Tomorrow is Friday. I will take you out there, and you will not have to come back home until the next Friday." As happy as we were to hear this plan, Mama somehow sounded even happier.

The following afternoon, we climbed into the Plymouth with her. We each had our own grocery-bag suitcase filled with all the clothes and other things we needed for the week. Joe was even taking his very own flashlight.

When we got to Grandma's house, there was another surprise awaiting us. Two of our cousins, Andy and Kay, were going to be there at the same time. There would be four of us to play together for an entire parentless week.

Andy and Kay were our nearest cousins, both in age and in where we lived. Their mother was our aunt Eddie, Mama's next younger sister. They lived only seven or eight miles from us out at Jonathan's Creek and were even closer to Grandma's house than we were.

Kay was ten years old, I was nine, Andy was eight, and Joe was nearly seven. We were set. Four cousins—three boys and one girl. This was the setup for the week.

The very first day we were there, the three of us who were boys isolated ourselves from Kay and would not play with her. She complained first to us, then to Grandma. Grandma's advice was simply, "Work it out."

Three boys had no interest in working it out. Our main activity that day was writing a special song to sing to Kay. We worked hard on it, and when we got it just right, we began to sing it to her over and over again:

> Boys are smarter than girls are,
> Boys are smarter than girls are,
> Boys are smarter than girls are!

That was the entire first verse. When we finished the first verse, we went on to the second verse:

> Boys are smarter than girls are,
> Boys are smarter than girls are,
> Boys are smarter than girls are!

There were more than two hundred verses to our song, and every one of the verses was just the same as every other. We loved it! Kay got so mad that she puffed up and turned red. She could not catch us, however, because we all ran from her in different directions.

After this kind of play went on for a day or two, Grandma was beginning to get tired of us. Suddenly, it was Monday morning. At breakfast, she made an announcement: "Today, children, is going to be a good day. Today is the day that the bookmobile comes from the library in town. Today, you may all go out to meet the bookmobile and check out books. That should keep you happy and occupied for the rest of the week."

The bookmobile was a little green panel truck with sides that opened up, revealing built-in shelves of traveling books. It came from the Haywood County Library in Waynesville. Every week, there was a schedule for travel all over the county to serve people who had no cars and had no way to get to town to check out books. We loved the bookmobile. It was summertime, a time when reading was encouraged at the library. And the summertime book limit was ten books per person. The four of us were going to end up with forty books for the week.

There was only one hardship: the bookmobile stopped up at the main road where Grandma and Granddaddy's farm road turned off at Rush Fork Gap. To get there, you had to walk a long mile back up the rough farm road to the paved road, then you had to carry the books all the way back.

Forty books was a number that we could not possibly successfully carry that mile back to the house. We complained to Grandma.

"I have already thought about that," she said. "The solution is on the way." She then went into a storage shed behind the house and came out with a little wooden wagon that Granddaddy had made for our mothers when they were children.

"Here, take this. You should be able to haul all your books home at one time. But you have to be careful with it. Your grand-daddy made it, and both of your mothers played with it when they were little. I don't want any harm to come to it. Now, which one of you is smart enough to pull the wagon carefully?"

Smart enough! We had just heard the magic theme word of our song! The three boys immediately started singing, "Boys are smarter than girls are!"

With that, Grandma made her decision. She gave the wagon to the one girl, Kay, and we had to follow as we watched her pull the wagon up the road. We did all we could to annoy her, kicking up dust, sticking sticks under the wheels, actually sitting down in the wagon like she was going to give us a free ride the rest of the way. Kay was not a happy girl when we arrived at the waiting place for the bookmobile.

The little green panel truck arrived. Miss Margaret Boyd was in charge of the bookmobile while school was out for the summer. We all knew her, and she was actually Andy and Kay's aunt on the other side of the family. She opened up the sides of the truck and helped us reach the books we wanted. In no time, we had forty books checked out and loaded onto the little wooden wagon.

When we started back down the rough road, a problem developed. The little wagon had solid wheels, and it had very low sides on the wagon bed. With the load of forty library books, every time one of the wheels hit a big rock in the road, about half of the books would slide off the side of the wagon and land on the ground. The only way we could figure out to handle it was for me to get on one side of the wagon and Joe to get on the other side of the wagon and hold the books in place with our hands every time it came to a rocky place. It did work, but it left Andy wandering around with nothing to do.

We were about halfway back to the house when the road passed beside a big barn where Granddaddy fed his cows in the wintertime. Andy was poking around the front of the barn, and he happened to see a corncob on the ground. All the corn had been shelled from it; it was simply a bare, empty corncob that was minding its own business.

Andy reported later that he had heard the corncob speak to him. He told us that it spoke to him and clearly said, "Throw me!" So he picked up the corncob and threw it at his sister. He missed, and the corncob fell beyond her on the ground.

He then went over to where the corncob had landed so he could pick it up and throw it again. That is when he discovered that the corncob had not landed on the ground. No, it had stuck up right in the middle of a pile of brownish stuff that one of Granddaddy's cows had deposited on the ground.

So Andy reached down, grabbed the clean end of the corncob, stirred it around a bit, then pulled it out and again threw it at Kay. This time, his aim was perfect. He hit her square between the shoulders.

All of a sudden, all of us began to notice things we had not noticed before. Right there in front of the big cow barn, there was a gigantic pile of corncobs, and Granddaddy's cows had been almost everywhere. In no time, a full-scale battle broke out.

We all understood that battles are pointless unless you have opponents and sides. So we divided ourselves into two armies. One army was made up of three boys. The other army was totally composed of one girl. The fight was under way.

We would grab the corncobs from the big pile by the barn, swirl them in the cow-pie ammo, and be ready to throw. The three of us boys surrounded Kay and threw at her from all sides while she desperately tried to grab anything to throw back at us. We did not even realize that, encircling her, when we missed, we most of the time then hit one another. In no time, we were all a terrible mess.

Soon, our battle degenerated into laughter. All four of us got the silly giggles. We had never made such an overall delightful mess. Andy and Joe and Kay and I all four staggered around laughing until we were crying and falling on the ground. Kay laughed harder than anyone.

Kay was laughing so hard that, as she once bent over, she split her pants. At that moment, for her, nothing in the world was funny anymore. The other three of us thought that this was funnier than ever. We were out of control.

Kay started trying to run backwards down the road, holding her split pants together, hoping she could get to Grandma's house and escape from us. We followed her, continuing to toss the last of the corncobs as we went. She was calling all of us a variety of interesting names along the way.

When we got close to Grandma's house, she was out on the front porch sweeping. She stopped sweeping and stood there, watching our scene with amused amazement. As Kay arrived, Grandma asked her, "Oh, little sister, what in this world happened to you?"

Kay told her the entire story, with three boys as the guilty characters.

With no bathroom, there was no easy way for us to clean ourselves up. Grandma herself took care of that. After our clothes were removed and discarded, we were each subjected to a cold-water-in-the-tin-tub bath with our grandmother scrubbing us using a brush so rough you could have taken the paint off a car with it. The bath itself was serious punishment.

While we were getting into new and dry clothes, I heard her ask Kay, "Why do you even play with those mean little boys?"

The answer was simple: "They are the only things here to play with."

"Then," Grandma smiled, "you are going to have to get smart enough to take care of yourself!"

When we were all settled, other questions came: "Children, I thought you went to get library books. Did you? Where are they, and where is my little wagon?"

We had totally forgotten about the library books. Heading back up the road to where the wagon had been abandoned, we discovered what had happened. The little wagon, with forty library books falling off the sides, had been right in the middle of our battlefield. Many of the books what had been one color when we checked them out had now become a new color. They looked like a terrible mess. We tried to wipe them off on the grass before taking them all down to the house, but they smelled terrible.

Even Grandma noticed. "I have never read a book before that had a smell to go with it."

We hoped it would fade away.

The rest of the week was calmer. We played each day, and gradually each read most of the books that had been rescued.

On Friday, a new announcement came from our grandmother: "Today, children, the bookmobile comes back. Since you will be going home before it comes again, I believe that you had better take your books back and turn them in today. Now, who is smart enough to pull the wagon on the trip back?"

We could not resist. The three of us boys started instantly singing again, "Boys are smarter than girls are!" We were unstoppable.

Instead of an objection, we heard a strange sound from Kay in the background. She was whimpering, "They're right, Grandma. They are smarter than I am. They can just take the old wagon. I am not even smart enough to go back up there with them. They can take it, and I will stay here with you!"

We felt wonderfully victorious. We had not only won the rights to the wagon, we had disposed of the girl. This would be a very pleasant trip.

Andy, Joe, and I loaded the books and pulled them all back up the road. We got to the big road just before the bookmobile got there. Our plan was to drop the books into the return box and run.

We did not get away with that plan. Miss Margaret Boyd knew that something was up, and she collared all three of us. She began to look at the books and smell each of them. The forty books were divided into two piles. Then she pulled out a sheet of paper and wrote our three names at the top. She made a long list on the paper and added a note at the bottom. Then she sealed it in an envelope and told us to take it to our grandmother.

When we got back to the house, Grandma and Kay were sitting on the porch talking and laughing and stringing beans. We handed the envelope to Grandma. She read us the message inside:

Dear Zephie,

When your three grandsons returned their library books, I discovered that twenty-two of them had been damaged beyond repair. I am afraid that they must be paid for so that they may be replaced.

It took me fourteen weeks of my total allowance to pay my

part of the bill. I do not know how long it took Andy, but Joe was broke at least as long as I was.

And Kay, the one girl . . . she did not have to pay a cent. Her name was not on the letter because she had been "not smart enough" to go with us to return the books.

After supper that night, when the three boys were bringing in wood for the cookstove and Kay was helping Grandma finish washing the dishes, we could hear the two of them softly singing together over and over again:

> Girls are smarter than boys are!
> Girls are smarter than boys are!

Chapter 7

THE LITTLE RAT

From kindergarten days, I was interested in science. The world seemed to be filled with experiments waiting to be performed. Nothing was more fulfilling than learning about how things worked, what would break or not break, what might burn, whether something could be flushed if you needed to get rid of it. I loved the world as my laboratory.

By the time I was no more than six years old, I already had three organized and named chemistry labs. One was called "the kitchen." The others were called "the bathroom" and "out in the garage." Nothing was more educational than experimental mixtures and combinations.

It was shortly before Christmas the year I had turned seven. Mama and Joe and I were in town at Bill Cobb's Firestone Store looking at toys and possible presents. Joe and I did not miss a thing. Our lists of wants were getting longer.

All of a sudden, I saw something that I had no idea they actually made for children. It was a real, deliberate, and so-named

Chemistry Set. The box was large and rectangular and had wonderful pictures on it of test tubes and burners and two children with smiling faces who were actually mixing chemicals. I was thrilled.

I called to Mama. "Look at this!" I pointed eagerly. "This is exactly what I have been needing. A chemistry set. Oh, if I could have this for Christmas, I would not even ask or hope for anything else." I thought that to be a very reasonable deal.

My schoolteacher mother said nothing. She simply came over and read everything that it said on the Chemistry Set box. Then she smiled at me and said, "I'm sorry. But it says you have to be ten years old to have this. You are simply not old enough." And that was it.

So I had to be content with my old chemistry sets: kitchen, bathroom, and garage.

Then, one wonderful day early in the following summer, I made a great discovery. Right there in our house, set up and waiting for me to use, was another chemistry set. I still do not know why I had never noticed it before. It had been there all the time. It was called "my mama's makeup" and was all lined up on the glass top of what she called her "blond dresser," complete with a little benchlike stool for me to sit on and a big, round safety mirror on the back of the dresser. (I called it a "safety mirror" because you could watch in it while you were experimenting and see in advance if anyone was coming up behind to catch you.)

This was the whole picture: Mama loved to buy makeup and then save it because it was so expensive. There was a census of makeup on that dresser, some of which went back for a full generation.

She would go to the store and buy a new box of bath powder. After she was back at home with the powder, the ritual would start. I would watch. She would open the new powder box, slit the paper that was protecting the powder, then take the powder puff and pat a little bit of the powder on the side of her face. I knew what was coming next. "Oh," she would smile to herself, "that powder smells sooo good. It was so expensive. I am going to save it!" I knew right then that the new powder would get to be two hundred years old if I did not do something with it.

Next to the powder boxes was a whole community of lotion bottles. They were different shapes, different sizes, different colors. Some of them had little pumps on the top so you could pump out a sample of the lotion. One or two even had little rubber bulbs that you could mash down, with good results. Every one of the lotions smelled different from every other one. And not a one of them tasted like they smelled.

Beyond the lotions was a thicket of lipstick, each tube standing in the lipstick neighborhood like a little, stubby tree. When Mama would buy lipstick at the store, she would always choose two very similar colors so that one of them was sure to be "just right." She would bring the new lipsticks home to try them out. After opening the two tubes, she would make a little mouth shape with the side of her thumb and the edge of her forefinger and draw little red/pink lips with the new lipstick. The verdict was always the same: "It wasn't that color at the store." I knew immediately that this particular lipstick would never be opened again unless I did it.

On the right-hand side of the dresser lived the gathering of perfume bottles. There must have been a dozen of them, various heights and exotic names. Some of the perfume bottles were made of colored glass—some gold and one blue. Almost all of them had beautiful little caps that looked like small versions of crowns for miniature kings and queens. They were arranged in height order, like a little glass chess set.

I loved this new chemistry set. It was complete. There was no need at all to take anything into the bedroom with you when you went to experiment. It was all there. You could take the top off of one of the bath-powder boxes and turn it over, and it was a perfectly usable little mixing bowl. Into this bowl you could put various powders, lotions, globs of lipstick, a little perfume, and mix it all up to see what you got. There were even two little sets of mixing devices. Mama called them "emery boards" and "orange-wood sticks."

Right through the door beside the blond dresser was our one bathroom with its white toilet just inside. If you saw or even heard anyone coming, all you had to do was to step into the bathroom, scrape the mixture into the toilet, and flush. All was gone!

My favorite time to play with the makeup chemistry set was when Mama went outside to hang out the laundry. It felt safer knowing that she was outside the house while I was in her room.

We had a washing machine but no clothes dryer. The washer was a beloved Bendix with a front-loading door that had a big glass window in it. Joe and I loved it when Mama did a load of wash. We had no television, so we would watch anything.

Once the load was in the Bendix, Mama would call us: "Come on in here, boys. It's about ready to start. Bring your little chairs so you can sit and watch."

Joe and I would drag chairs in front of the washer. After a brief fight about which of us got to pour the Oxydol into the opening in the top and which of us got to pull the big knob to start the cycles, we would settle into our chairs and watch as we listened to the water pouring in.

Then the show would start. As the drum of the washer started to turn, we would point and call out, "There goes my pajamas.

There goes my checked shirt. There goes your socks with the ele-
phants on them. There they go!"

Our favorite part of the wash was the spin cycle. As soon as
the spin cycle started, Joe and I would jump up from our chairs
and hang on the top of the washing machine. It would vibrate and
dance, shaking both of us as we hummed out loud to enhance the
noise of it all. This was as good as a ride at the fair.

When the wash was finished, Mama would come with her
dishpan to get the wet laundry. The dishpan went on the floor as
the door was opened and the clothes came out. I would watch her
pull the wet clothes out and estimate the time it would take her
to finish hanging out this particular load. I was pretty good at it.

On one certain day, she finished the wash and pulled out
about a twenty-minute load to hang out. Joe was playing somewhere else on his own, so it was a perfect time to head to the
makeup chemistry laboratory. There was, in fact, an experiment I
wanted to repeat to see if it turned out the way it had before. One
of the very fragrant bath powders was a pale ecru color. The Jergens Lotion (which smelled like cherries and almonds but did not
taste like either of them) was white. I did not understand why, if
you mixed very pale powder with white lotion, then stirred them
up, the resulting glob was a darker brown color than the powder
had been to begin with. I had to figure this out.

I headed to the bedroom and set up shop. Soon, I had a big
and thick glob adhering to an emery board, stirring round and
round. It was as dark in color as ever. All of a sudden, I realized
something was wrong. The glob that I had created was so thick
and hard that I was not sure it would successfully flush when it
needed to disappear into the toilet. It needed to be thinned out.

After looking up and down the makeup reagent table, I made
a decision: add some perfume. A good dose of perfume should

thin it out very well. There were the perfumes, standing in line like volunteers in the army. It was my choice.

At the very end of the perfume family, there was a very small bottle. It had never been opened because there was a story that went with this particular bottle. My aunt Pat, Uncle Lee's wife, who lived in Richmond, Virginia, had gone to London, England, earlier that year to see the coronation of Queen Elizabeth. When she came back, we looked at her pictures with delight. We also were each the recipient of a present she had brought to us from a big store in London she called "Harrods."

My brother's present was a little pair of folding scissors that even had a zipper case in which they lived and traveled. I was so jealous of this present. He could put the little scissors safely into his pocket, and everywhere he went he was ready and prepared to cut stuff.

She brought me a stupid-looking little pair of English sunglasses. They were black and pointy on the corners and had little jewels embedded in the plastic of the frames. They made me look like Elton John as a little boy. I never did wear them where anyone could possibly see me.

My daddy had gotten a little spade-shaped short necktie she said you called an "ascot." He didn't wear it either—said it would make him talk funny if he did.

Mama's present topped them all. It was a tiny box, beautifully wrapped. When she opened it, out came the little bottle of perfume. Mama read the label and gasped, "Chanel No. 5! Oh, how wonderful! I am going to save it!" I knew right then that the little bottle of perfume would never be opened unless I did it.

The Chanel No. 5 bottle was gold see-through glass. You could see the perfume inside. It did have a little crown for a top. I thought it very beautiful.

I picked up the bottle and easily unscrewed the lid. My bet was that Mama had opened it and sniffed it a lot, even though she had never put one single drop on her body. This was going to be great. After shaking a good little bit of the Chanel No. 5 onto the glob I had made, I stirred it around some more. Just as I had hoped, the added perfume smoothed out the mixture until there would be no trouble flushing it when the time came. And it all smelled great!

I had just put the little perfume bottle back in its home place when something caught my eye. Even though the glass of the bottle was gold in color, it was very transparent, and you really could easily see through it. Now that about half of the perfume was gone, there was a clearly visible line right at the middle of the bottle. It seemed to underline the words, "Chanel No. 5," which made it even more visible. Anyone, especially Mama, who looked in this direction would instantly see that someone had poured out half of the little bottle.

How to fix it? Fill it back to the top with water and make it again be full, or simply empty the rest and get rid of the telltale line in the middle? An easy choice. I picked the little bottle back up, unscrewed the lid, and dumped the rest into my mixture. It made it smoother than ever, and now the bottle drew no visual attention at all.

While all that was happening, my attention had relaxed, and somehow Mama had slipped back into the house unnoticed. She smelled it from the kitchen. When my mama came charging into the bedroom, she was not walking. She was on a flat-out trot. With one look at what I was doing, she grabbed me by the arm. To this day, that arm is slightly longer than the other, as she yanked me into the air, trying to ignore all simple laws of gravity. She spun me around and popped me down onto the little bench, now facing her. Her eyes were red and bulging. The powder-box lid fell from my hand, and everything spilled as it hit the floor.

I knew what was coming next, for I had been in this position before. I could hear the words before they came out of her mouth. "Mister," she would start out. "Mister, you *march* outside"—why did you have to "march" instead of walk whenever your mother was mad at you?—"go up to my switch bush, and get your own switch. And it better be a good one!"

There was one bush in the backyard that Daddy was not ever supposed to trim. It was Mama's switch bush. It was a kind of privet hedge that had long stems of flexible new growth she thought made the perfect device for punishment. The entire ordeal was that you had to go to the bush and select a long, thin branch. Then you had to carry it back to where she was waiting. She would take the switch and swish it around to see if it met her specifications. (If you tried to get one that was thin or weak enough that it would not hurt, she would surely send you back on a second trip to get another one.) Then she would strip off the leaves. She would make you hold up your britches legs (that was as much so that you couldn't run as that you now had bare legs), and she would, as she said, "stripe your legs" with the switch. The process was worse than the pain.

On this particular day, however, that exact request did not come. No, I seemed to have overdone things this time. Mama looked straight at me and talked to me with her pointed finger. "You sit right here and do not move while I go get the switch!"

I was terrified. I knew that she must be going to get a special switch that she had been feeding and training since before I was born. It might just be a whole tree. I could be going to die.

Once Mama left the room, I felt much calmer. Now, it was time to figure out what really needed to be done before she got back. I thought deeply about what was happening. I was about to die over a pitiful little bottle of never-used perfume. It was not fair. I simply was not willing to do that. That is when the idea came.

Sometime earlier, my cousin Andy had been spending the day with me when he got out of sorts, got a bad case of the pouts, and ran away. Mama searched everywhere for him. She went all over the inside of the house, then all over the yard, then through the garden and chicken lot and cow pasture, then all over the barn, then through all the bushes and trees that might hide him. He was nowhere to be found.

Over an hour later, she finally found him hiding in the garage behind the Mehaffeys' house, across the road and a few hundred yards below our house. When she finally found him, she was so exasperated that she sat down and cried, right there beside the well in the Mehaffeys' backyard.

Remembering this day, I now knew what to do. I was going to run away. Then Mama would have to put down the switch and look for me. When Daddy came home, she would have to explain to him why he did not have a little boy any longer. Then she would *cry*! It would be wonderful.

It was such a good overall plan that my brain went on to get one good idea too many. Suddenly, I realized that if I actually ran away, I would not get to watch her cry. And what good would it do to make her cry if I did not get to watch? I wanted to watch.

The plan made itself. I opened the back door of the kitchen, so it would look like someone had just gone out that way. Then I crawled into a little, low closet that was beside the stove in the kitchen. It was the place where the milk bucket lived, the place where kindling wood for the stove was kept. There was also a mop and broom in there. Once the door was pulled shut, I could look out through a wide crack and see everything in the kitchen. I was going to get to watch Mama cry.

Suddenly, the side door opened, and there she was. The switch she had brought looked like it was as alive as a snake. It was big, too. I hoped that she would not drop it on the floor because I knew it was capable of searching me out and killing me all on its own without any help from Mama.

All of a sudden, she saw that I was not seated where she had left me. She looked from the bedroom door all around the kitchen. "Where are you?" was Mama's question. "Where are you?"

I decided not to answer. She needed to find out on her own.

My mother walked over to the open door and looked out. "Did you go out of this house when I told you not to move?" Her voice was loud.

I still did not answer. *Go out and see*, I thought to myself.

She did. I could hear her calling for me as she walked all around the house. I was not there! Once back around to the door, she came back inside. She did not look good. Her eyes were already red, and I could hear her sound like she was struggling to breathe. *It is working*, I thought.

Mama picked up the receiver of the black kitchen-wall telephone and called a number. It was the number for Daddy at the bank. He came on the line. "Come home!" she was pleading. "He has run away, and I cannot to save my life find him. I have looked everywhere. Come home no matter what you are doing. . . . Yes . . . yes"—she seemed to be answering questions I could not hear—"yes . . . Well, maybe I did get too mad!" She hung up the phone.

Mama sat down at a chair at the kitchen table and put her head down on her folded arms. She was almost heaving as she breathed. This was getting better and better all the time.

In no time, Daddy's car came in the driveway. I heard the car door open and then slam. He was on the way inside.

The next few moments were like a scene from an opera. The door opened and my daddy stood there, tall and erect. Mama looked up at the sound of the opening door. She saw him. She seemed to lift into the air without any means of support whatever and with a high-pitched humming sound—"Uuuuuuuhhhhh!"—she flew through the air to meet him. She draped around his neck, sobbing. It was beautiful!

Daddy was not impressed. He looked down at her wet face and suggested, "Dry up! Let's go and look for him."

Mama wiped her eyes and face and joined Daddy at the door. They both went outside. I could hear them circling much farther around the house than the trip Mama had made on her own. They were searching beyond the garden, behind the chicken house, below the barn—everywhere I might have hidden if I had actually gone outside. Finally, they gave up and came back to the house.

When the two of them entered the door, Daddy was in the lead. He looked back at Mama over his shoulder and offered, "I am calling the police. This is a case for the police."

All of a sudden, I realized that I had not counted on this turn of events. I had not planned on the police being called. I was pretty certain that the police were probably not going to cry. It seemed to me like it was time to come out.

I pushed on the inside of the door. It did not budge. It was a little, undersized closet that had no doorknobs or normal latches. No, all it had was a little spring latch that snapped locked on the outside when you pushed—or, in my case, pulled—the door shut. There was no access to the latch from the inside. I was caught!

I thought about what to do. Then, very politely—yes, very

politely—I knocked three times on the inside of the closet door.

Mama heard the sound. "What was that?" she asked Daddy.

"What was what?" he responded. He honestly had not heard the knocking.

Before she answered him, I knocked again, three times.

Daddy heard clearly this time. "Well," he drawled, "it sounds like we've got a little rat in the closet! That's exactly what it sounds like."

Mama started to smile, though I could not figure out why. "How about that?" She looked at Daddy. "A little rat in the closet. Well, we surely do not want rats in our closet. What do you think we should do about it?"

Daddy was thinking about it. I could see him through the crack of the door. "We could mix up some poison and slide it under the door on a piece of bread. But if he is a smart little rat, he would never eat poisoned bread.

"I know what let's do," he went on. "I will go get my big gun and shoot through the door!"

With that, I started screaming and banging on the door at the same time. "*Nooo!* Nooo! It's me! It's me. It's not a little rat. Don't shoot, don't shoot!"

Mama came over to the outside of the door. She did not open it. She simply squatted down by the outside of the door and asked, "What's your name, little rat? Do you have a name?"

"Donald Douglas Davis is my name. You ought to know that! You gave it to me. Please let me out of here!"

Mama seemed to turn back toward Daddy and asked, "Donald Douglas Davis . . . ummm . . . Do we know anyone by that name?"

Daddy chuckled. "Not that I can remember right now. Stay here, I'm going to get my big gun!"

Through the years, I have wondered: was it legally child abuse for the two of them to sit there on the outside of that little closet door and laugh their heads off for a full ten minutes while I screamed and banged for my life on the inside of that closet door? It seemed like it lasted for an hour.

At last, Mama came over and opened the closet door. I was so exhausted and hyperventilated that I purely rolled, gasping, out into the kitchen floor, sobbing all the time, "I'm not a little rat, I'm not a little rat."

There was no punishment. I guess that everyone in charge thought there had been enough suffering for everyone.

After that day, two memorable things did happen.

The next time my aunt Pat came for a visit, my mama told her, "Pat, I want to thank you again for that lovely little bottle of perfume you brought me from Harrods. I have enjoyed it so much!"

With that, Aunt Pat questioned, "You mean that you have opened it?"

"Opened it?" Mama corrected, "Why, I have used every drop of it. And I have never had a bottle of perfume that gave me as much pleasure as that one!"

And that Christmas, even though I was only eight years old, I got the big chemistry set for Christmas . . . with a promise that I would play only with it and not touch another single thing in our house.

Chapter 8

RESPONSIBLE

M y grandmother had her first heart attack when she was in her fifties. All through my growing-up years, she had a series of heart attacks until "Grandma had a heart attack" was not an event of new crisis but almost part of the norm.

Each time she had a heart attack, part of the recuperation included spending a week or more at our house in town before she returned home to Rush Fork. This was almost like a party, as it meant suspension of normal household routine and rules. It was a treat to have Grandma in recovery with us.

The only problem with having our grandmother at our house she caused for herself. She was supposed to do something that the doctor called "rest," and she did not know the meaning of the word. We would leave her at home while we went to school and Mama and Daddy went to work. When we got home each afternoon, Grandma would have washed the clothes, cleaned the house, and cooked supper for the family. She could not bring herself to rest.

One day, Daddy told us that he had an idea that would help Grandma. He told us all about it at the supper table. "I have been thinking. It is so hard for Zephie to get any rest around here when we are all gone to work and to school. I have been thinking that if we got a television set, she could sit on the sofa in the living room and watch television, and she would get better more quickly."

We all knew that Daddy had been thinking about the television set for a long time. He was the one who wanted it, but Grandma was his excuse to be able to justify getting it at last.

He must have made a trip to Massie Furniture the next day because, at our next night's supper, we got the new chapter in the unfolding television story: "Tomorrow, it is coming!"

"What's coming?" Mama was not easily cooperating.

"Our new television set. The arrangements are all made. While we are gone to school and work tomorrow, two men from Massie's will come and bring the television set. Zephie, you must be on the lookout and let them in. They will put our new television set in the living room and hook everything up so we can try it out tomorrow night."

I could hardly sleep that night. The next day, I could not pay attention in school. No one in our family had a television set. I had never actually seen one turned on except in the window at Massie Furniture Company. Now, we were going to have one.

When we got home that day, we all knew it had happened. The moment Mama turned in the driveway, we could see it: the big silvery television antenna that was attached to the chimney on the top of our house.

"I hope that Santa Claus doesn't get hung up in that thing!" Joe worried.

Mama just laughed. "We will all have to get used to it, including Santa Claus."

We almost ran inside the house to see. Grandma was sitting calmly in the living room watching the television set. Mama and Joe and I joined her and carefully studied the big, square piece of furniture with the glass television-screen front. We watched and watched the television, not yet able to imagine what would happen when it actually got turned on. That would have to happen when Daddy got home, as none of the rest of us had any idea how to start up the thing.

Daddy got home and began to explain the television set to us like he was an expert. He walked us around the house and pointed out the arms and extensions on the silvery antenna. He showed us how the double wire came from the antenna down the side of the house and under the window into the living room. He showed us how the antenna wire was attached to the back and told us that the pictures would come invisibly through the air and then down the wire to appear on our own television. Then he told us that we would not have to wait; we would come into the living room and turn on the television set right after supper that very night.

I could not eat. I could not swallow. The excitement was too great. Finally, we declared ourselves fed and the family, including Grandma, adjourned to the living room. Daddy gave us all instructions about what to do so that the television could be turned on: "Everybody get a seat. Sit where you can see the screen, but don't get too close to that thing or it will put your eyes out." He turned all the lights off in the living room except for one lamp in the back of the room.

"Now I can't see." Joe voiced his concern. "It's too dark to see the television set."

"Hang on," Daddy returned. "You will be surprised!"

He picked up the plug and plugged in the television. (He had told us earlier that you had to unplug the television when it was not turned on so that if lightning hit the antenna it would not ruin the television.) We only got one channel: Channel 13, Asheville, North Carolina, ABC.

When he turned it on, we heard a humming sound. Then a bright spot appeared in the center of the screen and broadened into a horizontal line, and in no time we saw a picture on the screen.

The program was called *John Daly and the News*, and it was boring. Mr. John Daly was telling about President Eisenhower playing golf with somebody. I was disappointed in television.

All of a sudden, there was a break in the news program, and there appeared on the screen a little cartoon beaver holding a toothbrush. The little beaver had enormous teeth, and, while brushing his teeth with the toothbrush, he began to sing:

> Brusha, brusha, brusha, get the new Ipana,
> Brusha, brusha, brusha, it's dandy for your tee-eeth!

Now, this was something worth watching! Joe and I danced around the room while the beaver, who was now identified as "Bucky," finished his tooth-brushing song.

"Now, that was good!" I offered.

"That is what's called a 'commercial.' They are just trying to make us buy something," Mama filled us in.

I couldn't figure out why we did not go straight in the bathroom, throw away our half-used Colgate, and head to the store to get Ipana toothpaste.

Pretty soon, the news program came to an end. There was another wonderful commercial with a little character called "Speedy Alka-Seltzer" singing about, "Plop-plop, fizz-fizz . . ." I loved television.

All of a sudden, the program changed, and we saw a big man in a shiny suit holding a microphone. He was standing in the middle of what looked like a boxing ring and was surrounded by a horde of screaming people. "Welcome," the man shouted into the microphone, "welcome to *Champions of Texas Wrestling!*" We were simply hypnotized.

The announcer told us that the upcoming match was to be between two wrestlers called "the Little Swede" and "the Swamp Monster." He went on to tell us that the Swamp Monster was so ugly that a law had been passed that he had to wear a mask to appear in public or he would scare people to death! Out came the masked wrestler, and the entire audience booed.

Then the Little Swede was brought out. He was not so little after all, especially in the belly. He had long, stringy blond hair and wore trunks that looked like they were made out of spotted leopard skin. The audience all cheered wildly.

A bell rang, and the wrestling match began.

In no time, it was obvious to me that the Swamp Monster was a cheater. Every time the referee was not watching, the Swamp Monster would grab the Little Swede around the neck from behind. While he held him around the neck with one fat arm, with his other hand he bored his knuckles into the Little Swede's eyes and tried to blind him.

All of a sudden, Grandma jumped up from the sofa and started poking the television screen with her finger. "Cheater! Cheater! Cheater!" she screamed. "Catch him, stop him, don't let him do that!" She was hollering at the referee right through the television set.

Now, Mama jumped up. She ran across the room and jerked the cord out of the outlet in the wall. The screen collapsed in blackness until only a point of fading light glowed in the center. All was in quietness.

Mama looked sternly at Grandma. "Sit down, Mother! Sit down right now and behave yourself. We got this television to help you rest, not to fire you up and get you more out of sorts than ever. If you do not want us to take it back to the store, you will have to stop acting younger than the children and behave yourself."

Grandma slinked back to the sofa like a disciplined dog. She sat quietly, then almost begged, "Turn it back on. I won't do anything."

Through the rest of the Texas wrestling show, Grandma sat beside me. Her breathing was heavy, and I could hear her quietly whispering to herself, "Cheater, cheater, cheater."

A few days later, it was Saturday. Mama and Daddy were going to Asheville, and Joe and I were left to stay with Grandma. As soon as they were gone, the three of us unanimously headed to the living room and plugged in the television set. When it came on, we were all thrilled. It was Saturday-morning cartoons. There were Betty Boop and Popeye. Best of all were episodes of *The Little Rascals* and *The Three Stooges*. Grandma joined us as we acted like Moe, Curly, and Larry on our own after the show came to an end. We had a good time, but even with that, cartoons were still not as good at Texas wrestling.

Grandma had been with us for two weeks when the day came for Mama to take her back to the doctor's office for her checkup. Joe and I were not considered old enough to leave at home alone, especially with the unguarded television set, so we were popped into the car to go along for the ride.

The doctor's office was in the Medical Arts Pharmacy Building, a new building located just across the street from the Haywood County Hospital. The bottom level was the big, new drugstore, with the doctors' offices being the occupants of the second floor.

As soon as Mama pulled into the parking lot, we began to hear her plan: "Boys, I know that there is nothing for you to do in the doctor's office but get bored. And I don't want to leave you bored in the waiting room when I go back in there with your grandmother to talk with the doctor. That would be dangerous.

"So here is my idea. You boys go out there to the corner where the red light is, wait until all of the traffic is stopped, cross the street very carefully, and play in the big yard of the hospital until I come out there to get you. There are lots of trees, and there is wonderful shade over there. The dogwoods are blooming, and it will be a nicer place for you to spend time than being stuck over here in the doctor's office."

We thought it was a wonderful idea. Springtime was no time to be stuck indoors anywhere, especially in a stuffy old doctor's office.

As soon as we got out of the car, Joe and I were both ready to go. Joe got the first idea: "We could play Texas wrestling."

Mama was quick. "Absolutely not! Play does not mean horse-play. You boys sit under the trees and play quietly and safely. No Texas wrestling!"

Mama got Grandma out of the car, and they started toward the building. My brother and I headed down toward the protected crossing of the traffic light.

Just before we were out of Mama's sight, she gave us one last word: "Remember, Donald, you are the oldest. So you are responsible for your brother! Be careful and play calmly. We do not need another member of this family in the hospital." And we were gone.

Those horrible words "You are responsible" were left hanging in the air as Joe and I crossed the street, and he was making sure that I did not accidentally forget them.

"You're responsible, you're responsible, you're responsible," he grinned as he chanted over and over again. I already wanted to wring his little neck.

As soon as we arrived at the big lawn of the hospital, my brother proceeded to torment me. He would climb to the top of the highest tree, crawl out on a limb, and act like he was going to fall out, all the while calling to me, "If I fall, it will be your fault. You are responsible!"

I almost cried, begging him to come back down. He came down from the tree and immediately proceeded to run around and around and in and out through the cars in the little hospital parking lot. I should have anticipated his words: "If I get run over, it will be your fault! You are responsible!" He was willing to suffer pain just to get me in trouble. Texas wrestling would have been a whole lot calmer than this.

I desperately tried to figure out what to do. Suddenly, I had an idea. "Joe! Let's play tag. I know a good, new version that we have never played. Want to try it out?"

His curiosity got the best of him, and he agreed. "What kind of tag is it?"

I was thinking as fast as I could. "It's called 'Texas Wrestling Tag.' Do you see all of the dogwood trees that are in bloom?" He nodded his head in assent. "Well, those trees are the safety zones. If you are touching one of them, it is like you are on base. But they are only safety zones while the other person counts to ten. When the other person counts to ten, you have to let go and try to make it to another dogwood before you get tagged. If you get tagged, then you are 'it' and you have to do the chasing.

"Now, you are the Little Swede, and I am the Swamp Monster. See if you can catch me before I get to a dogwood tree, and you will win the first round of the wrestling match."

He agreed. I let Joe easily catch me. That would get him

interested in staying in the game. In fact, I let him catch me two or three times in a row so he would think he was good at this. Pretty soon, however, I was running hard, getting away, and always catching him.

He was holding on to a dogwood tree, puffing and panting, and I was counting to ten. On ten, he let go and began to run toward another far-off dogwood tree. I was hot on his trail. As he neared his goal, I yelled, "Swamp Monster's coming!" and growled at him like an enraged wild animal. He could not resist. He looked back, still running full speed toward the dogwood tree.

When he hit the tree, he had almost turned his head back around. So it was the side of his face that took the major part of the impact. His face hit the rough tree trunk a glancing blow, and he fell to the ground. When I got to him, he did not look normal. One side of his face was as it had always been. The other side looked like bloody, fresh hamburger meat.

Joe was crying, "You're responsible, you're responsible. This is all your fault!"

I begged him, "Don't cry. It will be all right. Don't cry! The Little Swede isn't supposed to cry!" Every time I uttered the words "Don't cry," his volume doubled.

Some people we did not know were coming toward their car from the hospital. When they heard Joe squalling, they came over to see what was going on. They took one look at him, and the woman said to the man, "We better get this child some help. It seems like nobody is responsible for him!"

They disappeared back into the hospital. In no time, a man and woman, both dressed in white, came running. The man was pushing a wheelchair. They picked Joe up, put him in the wheelchair, and hauled him away. All I could do was follow. He kept crying, "That is my brother. He is responsible!"

We ended up in the emergency room. Our own doctor, Dr. Lancaster, came through the curtains. He knew both of us. He took my brother somewhere into the back and left me to wait.

That is where Mama eventually found us after searching everywhere from the drugstore to the parking lot. She had left Grandma in the car while she looked for us, and her worry about getting back to our grandmother probably saved us from having a scene right there in the emergency room. There was plenty of time for this later.

Joe came out from behind the curtain with Dr. Lancaster. One half of his face had been painted with some stuff Dr. Lancaster told Mama was called "gentian violet." He looked like half a normal boy and half a package of purple hamburger meat.

On our way home, Joe told us that he liked "that new purple stuff." He said it did not burn like iodine. Dr. Lancaster had sent a bottle of the gentian violet home with us, and Joe was carefully guarding it like it was his best friend.

We arrived back at home at about the same time that Daddy got home from work. He knew nothing about all of our adventures, so there was a lot to tell him. I meant to let Joe do most of the telling, but Mama seemed to think that she had a lot to say about the day also. Daddy listened with smiling interest.

We had supper, and when we finished our meal Daddy had something to say: "I think that there is only one thing left to do to make this day complete." Without explaining, he picked up the bottle of gentian violet from where Joe had left it on the cabinet.

I, of all people, should have known what was coming. It was very foolish for me not to put two and two together, knowing my father as I did. He sat me in a kitchen chair and handed the gentian violet to Joe. He then asked Mama for a bunch of Q-tips. About then, I figured it out, but it was too late.

"Well, son"—he was talking to Joe—"why don't you fix your brother so that anyone who sees both of you on the street this week will know that you are related?"

Joe then proceeded to decorate my face with the new purple medicine.

Grandma watched and then announced that we did not need to watch Texas wrestling on our new television that night. When we asked why, she replied that we did not need to watch television since I looked worse than the Swamp Monster, and I was right here in the house.

When I whined and complained about being painted, Joe had one comment to make: "You are responsible!"

Chapter 9

"WATCH WHERE YOU STEP!"

S unday was a day of predictable routine at our house. Breakfast was not hurried as on school days, and we had pancakes instead of eggs and bacon. Mama made the pancakes from her own recipe, and we added gobs of our own butter and our favorite, Log Cabin Syrup, from a small cabin-shaped can that she heated by placing it in a pan of hot water on the stove. Everything was predictable.

The most predictable thing about Sunday, however, was church. We *always* went to Sunday school and church.

But I never gave up. We would get to the breakfast table on Sunday morning, and I would ask, "Well, what are we going to do today?"

"What day do you think this is?" Daddy would question.

"It's Sunday. What are we going to do today?"

"We are going to church," Daddy went on.

"We went to church last Sunday."

"We are going again. Do you know that if we don't go, they won't have church?"

"Well"—now I had an idea—"why don't we stay home and give everybody a break?"

It did not work. We went every Sunday without fail. Before I was out of elementary school, I had a string of Methodist Sunday-school perfect-attendance pins that was longer than the lapel of my little Sunday suit.

Before we left for Sunday school each Sunday, Mama had her own routine. As she cleaned up from breakfast (she washed the dishes and Daddy dried and put them away), she was at the same time starting our Sunday dinner. By the time we were ready to leave, she had it all but ready to eat. It would then go into the refrigerator so that, as soon as we got home from the eternity of church, we would be almost ready to eat. It was a good plan.

I was about eight years old and Joe was nearing six when, one summer Sunday, we got home from church to a sad announcement from Mama: "I didn't start working on our dinner before we left for Sunday school today, boys. I am going to have to cook it all now. While I cook, you boys can go outside and play."

Joe and I both heard and understood those words clearly—"Go outside and play"—so we headed for the door.

Just as we got to the kitchen door, Mama said, "Where do you boys think you are going?"

The answer was simple; she had said it herself. "We are going outside to play."

"Not in your Sunday clothes, you're not!" I really wondered why mothers insisted that you be able to read their minds. She had said nothing in this world about clothes. "Go to your room and both of you put on something for play that cannot be hurt. Put your nice clothes away for next Sunday."

Joe and I went to our shared room. I said to my brother, "Something that cannot be hurt . . . ummm . . . I guess we'll have to go naked. They've never made clothes that can't be hurt."

After we both laughed, Joe and I took off our Sunday clothes and put them on hangers in the closet. Since it was summertime, both of us ended up putting on shorts and T-shirts. As always in the summer, we stayed barefoot, relieved to be out of the shoes we wore to church.

Now re-dressed and back in the kitchen, we asked Mama, "Is the food ready yet? We are about to starve."

"You're not going to starve," she countered. "You know it's not ready this soon. It takes a long time to cook Sunday dinner. You are going to have to wait. I know . . . I have a good idea about something you can do while you wait."

I knew that whatever she was thinking was going to be stupid. I didn't have any idea what it might be, but I certainly knew that it was going to be stupid.

"Why don't you boys go outside," she suggested, "and see how many times you can run around the house until I call you?"

It was stupid!

Joe and I couldn't think of anything better to do, so the two of us went out the kitchen door and started to run around the house.

Where we lived, on Plott Creek Road, we really were in the country. Behind our backyard was the chicken lot. As we rounded the corner below the house, we were running parallel to our own cow pasture. Turning into the front yard, we were just through the bushes from the gravel surface of Plott Creek Road, then . . . trouble. Just before we got to the side of the house where the little yard separated the house from Daddy's garden, we came to our own gravel driveway. Besides the basic gravel, it was also a place where Daddy dumped coal cinders in the wintertime. With bare feet, you could not run across there.

Actually relieved, we walked all the way back around to the kitchen door. Slouching in the door, we complained to Mama, "We can't run around the house. The cinders and gravel in the driveway, they hurt our feet. We can't do it!"

By that time, Daddy had taken off his necktie and was in the kitchen setting the table for all of us while Mama was in the middle of cooking. "I have an idea," he offered. "Don't try to run around the house. I couldn't do it either. Those cinders are sharp. So why don't you go back outside, climb over the fence, and run around in the cow pasture? There are no cinders and no gravel in the pasture. It is just nice, green grass."

Sounded great to us. We headed for the door before Mama had a different idea. As we went out the door, I barely heard Daddy caution us, "Better watch where you step!"

Joe and I were both pleased and excited. We didn't climb over the fence. Instead, we went to the back corner of the yard and went through the gate beside the chicken lot. It led directly into the corner of the pasture on the way to the barn. We only had one cow: a heavy Jersey milk cow Daddy had named Helen in honor of our nearest neighbor, Mrs. Helen Burgin, much to Mama's embarrassment. We only needed one milk cow, and the pasture was about large enough for one cow.

Joe and I both started running all over the place—no organized game, just running in crazy circles and chasing one another. After all, dinner would surely be ready very soon. Looking down as I ran, all of a sudden I remembered what Daddy had said as we left the kitchen: "Watch where you step!" I chuckled because I knew that he did not need to tell me that. I knew very well what was on the ground in the cow pasture (Daddy called them "sun cakes"), and I wasn't about to step in one.

About that time, Joe happened to come running in a circle in front of me. That's when I noticed his sweet little clean feet. And that is also when I got the idea for a science experiment.

"Joe, Joe, Joe," I called to him. "Stop running and come over here. I want to tell you something."

"What is it this time?" He was cautious. "I am not going to smoke another cigar."

"Nooo," I promised, "you have already done that. I just want you to think about something."

"What?" He was interested.

"What if you were running around and you just happened to step into a cow pile—you know, a sun cake. What do you think would happen if you did that?"

"I know what would happen," Joe frowned. "It would get all over your foot, and you would stink for the rest of your life."

"Maybe," I agreed. "Or maybe not!"

"What do you mean, 'Maybe not'?"

"Just think about it." I was leading him. "What if you were so fast—and I know that you are fast—what if you were so fast that you could step into a cow pile and pull your foot out so fast that there was not time for anything to get on it? What do you think about that?"

"Do you think it would work?" He was thinking about it.

"There's only one way to find out," I offered helpfully. "Let's try." But I knew very well I meant not, "Let's try." It was, "You try."

We looked around until we found a nice fresh one. It was nice and slicky-greenie looking on top. Then Joe got ready. He lifted his little six-year-old foot and came down, *Splaam!* It geysered up between his toes! It was beautiful!

"It didn't work," he lamented with real sadness.

I took care of him. "Don't worry. That's just your first try. You don't expect to get anything perfect on the first try. Do it again!"

He did it again. This time seemed to splash as high as his head. When I looked at him, he had a little grin on his face. He was beginning to like this.

"I'm going to try the other foot," was his solution.

He tried one foot, then he tried the other foot, then he ran and jumped with both feet. Sometimes, he slid down in the attempt. In no time, he was covered all over. I could only wonder how far away you could catch a whiff of his smell.

Just about that time, Daddy called from the house for us to come to dinner. We did not go toward the house. No. We went around and hid behind the barn. I remember thinking that I could actually live behind the barn. I didn't need a house. This would do very well.

After a few calls from the house, Daddy came looking for us. He came through the gate and across the pasture calling, "Boys! Donald, Joe! Where are you? Dinner is ready."

Joe was lurking just around the corner of the barn. When Daddy called his name again, he jumped out, arms spread, a big smile on his face. "*Ta-daa!* Look at me!"

Daddy almost fell over backwards. "Whoa! What in the world got a hold of you?"

My brother, Joe, seemed very happy with that question. He proceeded to tell Daddy the entire story of everything that had happened since we arrived in the pasture. I was the main character in the story.

Knowing my father, I would have soon guessed what was in his mind. There was no need to guess, however, because he immediately told me: "If you are so smart, you can now show him how it's done."

It then became my select privilege to be taken around by Daddy so that I could stomp every cow pile in the pasture. Twenty-six

I remember being fresh enough to merit attention. All the while, my brother was following along with his commentary: "It doesn't work. I knew it wouldn't work. See, it doesn't work...."

When we got back toward the house, Mama had walked out into the yard to see why we had been so slow in coming. She took one whiff/look at us and announced that our clothes had to be burned.

Joe started wailing, "I don't want to die, I don't want to die!"

"No, silly." She was smiling now. "You're not going to die. You take them off first."

So right there in the backyard of our house, where people riding down the road in cars could look at us, we had to take off all of our clothes until we were little naked boys in the yard. Daddy started spraying us with the water hose while Mama pushed the ruined clothes into a pile with a garden hoe. They would be burned later.

Then, while we were still being sprayed, Mama went back into the house. She returned a few minutes later with a big bucket of warm, soapy water and the mop. She and Daddy both laughed as she proceeded to mop us naked while he continued to rinse with the hose. It got to be fun. Joe and I joined in their laughter as we were tickled by both the mop and by Mama and Daddy's enjoyment of the end of our adventure.

We all had so much fun that we didn't stop until all the soapy water had been used up. Then Mama tossed us towels she had brought out to the porch, and we all went inside.

There was a burned smell in the kitchen. We had played in the water so long that our long-awaited Sunday dinner had burned. Mama didn't even get mad about it. She just threw out the burned food, and we all got in the car. Daddy took us to Charlie's Drive-In to eat.

After that Sunday, Mama tried very hard to be sure that Sunday dinner was well under way before we left for church. After that Sunday, I do not remember Daddy ever suggesting that we play in the cow pasture.

I decided that day that if we ever got another little brother in our family, we should all agree not to teach him to talk. That way, no matter what, he could not tell on me.

For a long time, it was not clear to me whether my brother, Joe, had learned anything that day. I actually thought he had not because he continued to do whatever I suggested—"Smoke a cigar," "Jump off the house with an umbrella," "Roll that ball out in the road and see what cars will do. . . ."

Eventually, however, I realized that he had learned a lesson I had missed: if he did something but I was the one who thought it up, he was not the one who paid for it. No, just like in the cow pasture, he almost always had the last laugh on me.

Chapter 10

PIMENTO CHEESE

Mama was never involved in many social activities. From the time I was born until she started back to teaching school, she spent all of her time taking care of us and the household. When she went back to teaching, there was no time at all for optional organizations. She was, however, always a part of the Women's Society of Christian Service at the Methodist church.

The WSCS, as it was called, was organized into "circles," smaller groups of women who met monthly at various homes of members, where they had refreshments, exchanged community and personal information of importance, and occasionally had study programs. Mama was a faithful member of her circle.

I loved it when the circle meeting came around to being at our house. There was one reason: leftover refreshments. Mama always planned the refreshments with the assumption that every single member of the circle would surely be coming to the meeting. In reality, only about half of those on the roll showed up for any particular monthly meeting. She also thought that every woman coming would try each of the things she had to offer. This also was not true. While some of the ladies clearly gobbled down more than their share, some of them ate like birds. There was always an abundance of leftover refreshment material after the meetings.

When Joe and I were little and she was not teaching, Mama would make the refreshments on her own at home. But after she was teaching again, there was no time for this. No, now she bought the refreshments at Whitman's Bakery on Main Street in Waynesville.

I loved to go to Whitman's Bakery. Mr. Whitman was a balding, pale man with rimless glasses. I thought he was so pale because he lived in contact with so much white flour all the time. More than anything else that they made, I loved the filled cream horns most of all.

Mama did not buy cream horns for the circle ladies. No, for them, she got an assortment of cookies, always the same. She got dozens of tea balls, Danish wedding cookies, sugar cookies with sprinkles on top, and pecan cookies that had chopped nuts in them. I loved them all.

One Sunday, I read in the church bulletin that "Circle No. 3 will meet at the home of Mrs. Joe Davis." It made my mouth start watering right there in church. I knew that on Wednesday afternoon, we would be going to get the cookies at Whitman's and I might be able to beg a cream horn at the same time.

On Tuesday night, I thought that maybe I should be sure that Mama remembered the circle meeting so that she would not forget about the refreshments. "Mama, I guess we will be going to the bakery after school tomorrow for sure."

"What for?" She looked puzzled.

"To get ready for the circle meeting. I know that we will be going to Whitman's so Mr. Whitman can get together the refreshments you are going to need."

"Oh." She looked thoughtful. "I have a new plan for tomorrow. We are not going to have cookies for the meeting. No, some of the women are talking about going on diets and staying away from so much sugar. I have another surprise plan for tomorrow. I think everyone will like the idea."

That was all she was going to offer. There was no clarification, no further explanation. We were to be in the dark about the refreshment plan.

The next afternoon, Joe and I met her at the car for the ride home from school. We started for home but stopped right across the street from Ralph Summerow's Cash Grocery in Hazelwood. I knew that Mama was going to the grocery store at Ralph's because that is where we always shopped.

"You boys stay in the car," she ordered. "I will be right back." Then she looked straight at me. "You are the oldest, so you are in charge. Keep things under control, will you?"

Joe and I both knew why she did not want us in the store with her. This way, we were not going to have the opportunity to make any begging suggestions about what went into the grocery cart. The only good thing was that maybe she would finish shopping more quickly and not leave us in the car for what seemed like hours at a time.

She really was not gone long, and I was surprised that she had two large brown grocery bags full of stuff when she returned to the car. She handed the bags into the backseat but did not get in the car.

"You boys stay right here. I need to run into Josephine's Dress Shop and see about some shoes. I do not have one decent shoe to wear tonight." She looked straight at me and said it again: "You are still in charge." And she was gone.

This time, she did not come back quickly. She stayed and

stayed and stayed. I almost thought about going to look for her at the dress shop, but I knew that she would only fuss at me for being impatient, and it would then take her even longer to finish in the store. Joe and I waited.

We had no games to play. We had no books to read. You could not turn the radio on in the Plymouth without the key being turned on. We were stuck. We were also starving. Lunchtime at school always came early in the school day, and now it was almost four o'clock. I could hear my own stomach pleading for a snack.

I was in the front seat, and Joe was in the back, where the grocery bags had been stashed. Being in charge, I made the suggestion: "Let's look in the groceries and see if there is something we can eat so we won't die before we get home."

I climbed over the seat, and we inspected the contents of the two bags. I knew as soon as we looked into the first bag that this was the right thing to do. Right there was a very easy solution to our starvation problem, and it was one of our favorite things.

Across the street at Ralph's Cash Grocery, Lucy Summerow, Ralph's wife, made homemade pimento cheese that they sold in the dairy case of the store. We all loved Lucy's pimento cheese. Right there in the grocery bag, we found not one but two of the large-size containers of pimento cheese. Besides the pimento cheese, there were two loaves of Colonial Thin-Sliced Sandwich Bread and two loaves of light brown Roman Meal Bread. We were in luck!

Joe opened one of the loaves of Roman Meal Bread while I popped the top off of one of the large-size pimento cheese containers. I could take the cardboard lid of the container, bend it slightly, and use it to scoop out a large quantity of pimento cheese. Then, while Joe held the bread, I spread the cheese on one piece of bread, and he added a second slice of bread to the top. In only moments, Joe and I each were eating two fat pimento cheese sandwiches. It was delicious.

In no time, my brother and I had finished our first sandwich and were chomping our way through the second. That is when I had a wonderful idea: "If we go ahead and eat enough for it to count for our supper, Mama will not have to take time to cook for and feed us when we get home. That way, she can get ready for the circle ladies to come."

Memory is surely a tricky and malleable thing, but it seems now that we had at least four sandwiches each, finishing one entire large container of pimento cheese and almost all of a loaf of bread. We had done a good thing. I folded up the essentially empty bread package and put the lid back on the pimento cheese container just as Mama finally returned from Josephine's.

She had apparently been a successful shopper, as she was carrying a new shoebox under her arm as she approached the car. We didn't say anything at all as she got in because we wanted to happily surprise her.

"I'm sorry I took so long," she offered. "I just couldn't find exactly the right thing. I hope the ones I got are going to look good enough."

"I know they will be fine!" I offered encouragement.

We arrived at home, and Joe and I helped carry the groceries into the house.

"Boys, I am running late. Maybe I better fix the refreshments before I get some supper together. Do you boys want to help me do that? It is my big surprise."

We were happy to agree.

Once the bags were on the kitchen counters, Mama began to gather things she apparently needed for us to fix the refreshments. She got a big cutting board and put it on the kitchen table.

She got out several knives—some sharp, some not—and added them to the supplies. Then she opened a drawer and took out a little white cardboard box that we had never seen before. "This is the secret!" she announced.

When Mama opened the box, we saw that it contained what looked like four cookie cutters, except they were bigger than cookie cutters. If you had used them for cookie cutters, they would have made cookies as large as a slice of bread. And they were very interesting shapes. The four cookie cutters were shaped exactly like the symbols on the playing cards Mama and Daddy used when they got together with friends to play bridge or canasta. I knew what these shapes were called. They were called, "spade," "heart," "diamond," and "club."

I asked Mama, "What are you going to do with those big cookie cutters?"

"They are not cookie cutters," she smiled. "They are party sandwich cutters. You see, I got Lucy Summerow to make me a special fresh run of her wonderful pimento cheese. That's what I stopped for at the grocery store. I also got both white and brown bread.

"I am going to make special pimento cheese sandwiches for the ladies in the circle. You boys can help. We will use one piece of white bread and one piece of brown bread for each one. Then we will cut out the shapes. We can arrange them in a nice pattern on the big tray with some of the white sides up and some of the brown sides up. And boys, you can eat the scraps we trim off while we do this, and you won't get too hungry until I can fix you some supper."

I knew in that moment that there was nothing to be said. There was no excuse to be offered. There was no explanation that was worth even trying to state. And I knew that as soon as she reached into the grocery bags, the rest of this day would not have a happy ending.

I did the only thing I could think of to do. I excused myself like I needed to go to the bathroom and left the kitchen in a hurry.

I could hear Mama pick up the first brown paper grocery bag. Then I heard her first words: "What on the face of this earth has happened to my groceries? You boys have eaten up the very special things that I bought to serve to the circle ladies! What in this world am I going to do now?"

She must have been looking at Joe as she said this because he was quick to answer: "Don't look at me. I was not in charge!"

I had to move quickly, as there would not be much time before she came looking. I was at the telephone now, picking it up and dialing four-five-six-six-zero-six-one, the number where Daddy worked at the bank.

In a moment, he was on the phone. "What do you need?" he asked.

"Actually"—I tried to be quick without sounding hurried— "I am calling for Mama. She wants to know if you can stop by Whitman's Bakery and pick up cookies for the circle ladies. What she wants is two dozen each of tea balls, Danish wedding cookies, sugar cookies with sprinkles on them, and pecan cookies with chopped-up pecans in them, and six cream horns!"

Daddy laughed out loud. "I am almost on the way right now! Tell her I am glad to be helpful."

When Mama was really mad, she fell into the habit of asking questions she thought to be unanswerable, instead of making any statements with which you might argue. I had counted on this, and I was right.

She came into the room where I was in retreat. "Mister-in-charge! We are all in a mess now. Just what do you think can be done to take care of the refreshment situation before the circle ladies get here in less than one hour?"

I was ready. "It is already done! Since I was in charge, I called Daddy at the bank. He is on the way home right now, and he is bringing eight dozen fresh cookies and six cream horns!"

She actually looked relieved. Then she caught herself. "And what are we supposed to do with cream horns?"

"We don't need to do anything. Mister-in-charge will take care of it."

And I did.

Chapter 11

SOMETHING UP HER SLEEVE

B ack in the first grade, we were all in Mrs. Annie Ledbetter's room. Mrs. Annie Ledbetter was a jolly lady who laughed at almost everything we did and was a wonderful teacher for our first year of school.

One day I remember well was the first day of the month of February that first-grade year. It was a classroom ritual on the first day of each month for us to watch while Mrs. Ledbetter tore the calendar page of the old month off the Garrett's Funeral Home calendar, and we looked with delight at the new month that was waiting for us. She would point out special days to come, and everyone who had a birthday that month would get to come up and write their own name on that square of the calendar.

Mrs. Ledbetter went on, "For first-graders, the most interesting day this month is probably Saint Valentine's Day, and we need to start getting ready for it this very day. We need to make our Valentine's Day mailboxes today, so that all of you can begin to give Valentines to one another before we have a big party on that special holiday."

Mrs. Ledbetter then passed out red construction paper and white construction paper. She showed us how to fold the white construction paper and cut out sections of the folded paper with scissors so that, when you unfolded the paper and placed it over the red paper, you got wonderful decorative patterns. We were to make mailboxes that looked like decorated pouches and would hold Valentines.

We all folded our white paper as well as we could in imitation of what we thought we had watched her do. Now we were ready to cut, but disappointment was on the horizon. Mrs. Ledbetter passed out the stupid little blunt-nosed, loose-jointed scissors. Just as we tried to cut with them, the folded paper flopped over sideways and stuck between the blades of the loose scissors. By the time we got it unstuck, we were all so frustrated that we ended up tearing the white paper into messy sections with our own hands.

Besides that, she wouldn't let us use the stapler because we "might catch our fingers." Instead, she passed around a big jar of white paste that tasted a lot better than it stuck. It even had a little, flat wooden spoon in it just like you got with a Dixie Cup of ice cream. We all ate the paste in no time, and in the end she had to staple our mailboxes together herself so they wouldn't fall apart.

We wrote our names on the mailboxes as well as we could. Mrs. Ledbetter thumb-tacked them to the chalk tray along the bottom of the blackboard, and they were ready to receive mail.

As we left school that afternoon, she reminded us, "The mailboxes are now open, boys and girls. We will be careful to keep our door closed all through this time so no one can come in and take our Valentines. You have to watch out for things like that."

As soon as I got home, I reported on the day, and Mama took me down to the Hazelwood Pharmacy to get my Valentines. Hazelwood Pharmacy was not CVS. They did not have two entire aisles of Valentines and candies that had been set up since the day after Christmas. No, at Hazelwood Pharmacy, they had set up a small folding table that was not much bigger than a card table.

I walked up to the table and immediately started looking. There were some large individual Valentines, each sold with its own red envelope. They had things like little gold metal hearts glued to them and little bows tied through the card itself. You could run your fingers over the surface of the card and feel the raised shape of the flowers pictured there.

"How about these?" I suggested.

"Put those down," was the immediate reply. "Those are not for children. Those Valentines are for people who are going to get married or something."

I put them down like they were burning my fingers and went around to the other end of the table. There were slick cardboard books filled with pages that had Valentines printed on them. The shapes were perforated so that they could be punched out. There were no envelopes.

"What about these?" I tried again.

"Those are the cheapest ones. I think we can do a little better than that."

I was beginning to think that this Valentine business was more complicated than I had expected.

Mama directed my attention to the center of the table. There in the center was a large pile of red mesh bags. Whoever planned those little bags surely understood exactly how many children were in a North Carolina school classroom. There were twenty-eight little Valentines, each with its own red envelope, and one slightly larger Valentine labeled, "For my teacher."

We bought a bag of these Valentines and headed home for supper, to be followed by my own time to prepare Valentines to take to school the following day.

It took me all of about five minutes to finish. I picked out four of the Valentines very carefully. One had a bear on it and said, "To my friend." It was to be for Eddie Bryson. One had fire trucks on it. It simply said, "Happy Valentine." I addressed it to Harold Allen. The third one said, "Let's play!" and showed several children having what looked like a Valentine's party. It went to Eddie Curtis. The last one, for Bruce Bowman, had two dogs on it. It didn't have words on it, just red hearts over the dogs' heads and "Bow-wow" inside each of the hearts.

Since I was now finished, I started to put the rest of the Valentines away in the red mesh bag. This bagful would probably last me through elementary school.

Mama came walking through the kitchen and saw me put the last of the unneeded Valentines away. "What are you doing?" she asked in a very suspicious and accusing-sounding voice.

"I'm putting away the Valentines that I don't need. We won't even have to buy any next year."

Mama looked at the four I had addressed. Then she looked at me. "You must not understand how you are supposed to do Valentines," she started. "You have to fix a Valentine for every person in your classroom."

I almost fainted! This was the most ridiculous idea that I ever heard of. Was she crazy? Did she not know what the words on some of those Valentines said? They sounded like promises for life! Did she not know who all the kids were who were in my classroom? I was not going to ruin my life in the first grade. I refused.

Mama went on. She insisted that I take the Valentines back out and address every one of them, one to each of my twenty-seven classmates, while she watched like a policeman.

Now, my mother could make me fix the Valentines. She could make me leave home with them on the way to school the next morning. But she did not go all the way inside my classroom with me when I got to school.

By the time the morning bell rang, all of my Valentines had been mailed. Four of them were mailed in the proper mailboxes inside our classroom. The others were mailed in the trash can inside the boys' bathroom. I was taking no chances with overcommitment.

Finally, Valentine's Day came. Eddie Bryson's mama was the cupcake mama. She showed up that day with cupcakes we knew she had made sometime over the weekend. They were shriveled up with dried icing and had jelly beans that had half-dissolved down into the icing and bled red coloring halfway to the edge of the cupcake itself. But they were our only source of sugar at the moment, so we all ate a round of them with great appreciation.

As soon as the first round of cupcakes was finished, Mrs. Ledbetter made the announcement: "Boys and girls, you may now open your Valentine mailboxes."

We rushed the blackboard wall. No force on the face of the earth could have stopped what happened next. Some unidentified small voice yelled out, "Wheew! I got twenty!"

The next voice followed: "That's nothing. I got twenty-two!"

At the same time, Mrs. Ledbetter was foolishly waving her hands and saying, "No, no, boys and girls. That is not what Valentine's Day is all about. It does not matter how many Valentines you get. It is the spirit of the thing that matters!"

None of her words mattered at all to any of us. We knew in our little six-year-old hearts that the world was all about competition, and we seldom got a chance to enter into the game. This was our chance! We wanted to win. There was no stopping the classroom until every single one of us had had our chance to call out the counted number.

All of a sudden, the room fell silent. To be sure, no more numbers were being called out, but there seemed to be more to the silence than that. It was the kind of profound silence that pulls your eyes toward it, the kind of silence that is not caused by the absence of sound but by something so negative that it erases the movement of sound itself.

There, in the center of the silence in the back of the room, stood a little girl named Willie Freedle. Willie Freedle was a little dull-haired girl who came from way back up Allen's Creek. We watched in silence as Willie Freedle held her Valentine mailbox upside down. She was gently shaking it with one hand and with the other fishing up inside, trying to find something that was simply not there. Willie Freedle did not get one single Valentine.

About that time, we were interested in sugar again. To break the silence, someone asked about more cupcakes. Cupcakes came out, and we ate.

Since most of the class was more interested in sugar than in Valentines to begin with, we actually threw the majority of our Valentines into the trash can after they were counted. I can still to this day look back into my memory and watch, as we went out the door when the afternoon bell rang, little Willie Freedle. She was squatted by the trash can digging through the contents. Looking for some Valentines that had no names on them, she collected them, then slipped them into her worn and handed-down book bag. I knew even then that Willie was taking them home so she would have some help in trying to tell a story that night about all the things that had not really happened at school on Saint Valentine's Day.

Valentine's Day in the second grade was only slightly different from that in the first. We did have better scissors, and we got mucilage instead of white paste. The mucilage tasted terrible and you couldn't get the taste out of your mouth, but it did stick a little bit better. We also got to use the stapler to put our mailboxes together.

There was one other big difference. After Eddie Bryson's mama served the half-dried-up cupcakes, we opened our mailboxes and shouted out the numbers. This year, I got twenty-eight Valentines, because there were twenty-eight children in our total class and Eddie Bryson had taught me to give one to myself. It also turned out that Willie Freedle got two Valentines.

After what happened in the first grade, my mama and Eddie's mama found out about it. This year, both of them not only made us fix Valentines for Willie, they each walked us to school and led us into the classroom by our ears and made certain that the designated Valentines were properly deposited into Willie's mailbox.

Third grade was somewhat different. We were in Miss Metcalf's room this year. She was a new teacher, just out of college, and she had a lot of new ideas. We got to use doilies in addition to red and white construction paper in making our mailboxes. With doilies, scissors, mucilage, paper, and the stapler, we made mailboxes that today could have come from Victoria's Secret. Some of them draped from the chalk tray all the way down to the floor.

This year, Willie Freedle got three Valentines. Harold Allen's mama found out what was happening, and she pulled Harold in by the ear also.

In the fourth grade, we were in a different world. Our teacher this year was Miss Daisy Boyd. It was her fortieth year teaching fourth grade, and she taught, as she said, by "doing things instead of talking about them." We spent the year taking an imaginary trip around the world, a trip in which the places we pretended to go and the things we pretended to see were the context for shaping everything we learned, from spelling to arithmetic.

When the first day of February came, she started the day off with a surprising announcement: "Today, boys and girls, we enter a very special month. First of all, it is the shortest month of the year. I think it is made that way so that winter gets over sooner! It is also the only month of the year in which we have four holidays."

Miss Daisy was all excited about every holiday she could find. We knew that something special was coming.

"The first holiday in February is Groundhog Day. It is tomorrow. We will watch the weather carefully tomorrow to see whether we think that the old groundhog will see his shadow and give us six more weeks of hard weather."

At this time as we were traveling along on our imaginary trip, we happened to be in Italy. We asked Miss Daisy whether they had groundhogs in Italy. She told us that it did not matter because the groundhog about which we were concerned lived in North Carolina. It was the one that made our weather.

She went on with the holidays: "On February twelfth, we have Abraham Lincoln's Birthday. Then we have George Washington's Birthday on the twenty-second of this month. Two of our most important presidents were born during the same month, but not the same year, boys and girls.

"But my favorite February holiday comes before those two birthdays. It is Saint Valentine's Day. The old groundhog will take care of himself tomorrow, but we need to go ahead and begin to think about Saint Valentine's Day even today."

Later that very day, as we continued our imaginary travels around the world, we came into a little town which Miss Daisy told us was the very town in which a man later called Saint Valentine was born. That very day, she told us the entire story we had never, ever heard about the man from whom Valentine's Day got its name.

It was way back in the time of the Roman Empire, she told us. The emperor of Rome was having a hard time getting young men to join the army because they did not want to leave their young wives. So the emperor got a bad idea. He decided to make getting married against the law. That way, none of the young men would have any wives of any kind, so they would join the army and not have to miss them.

Even we knew that this sounded like a very stupid idea. Right then, we knew a lot about why the Roman Empire did not work in the long run.

Then, according to Miss Daisy, this man called Valentine came into the story.

He was a plain old priest who heard about what the emperor had done. He knew that this was a dumb idea, so Valentine performed marriages for young couples in secret. It turned out to be hundreds and hundreds of couples, and he showed the world forever, she said, that even the emperor of Rome can't stop love.

We heard the story, but we secretly talked among ourselves about two things. If Valentine was a priest, he was not married, so what did he know about love? And more important than this, Miss Daisy herself was not married, so how did she know? Or maybe Miss Daisy knew that love was about more than just getting married.

Miss Daisy's classroom was a strange and different place in many ways. We had no school library at Hazelwood School at this time. Miss Daisy's room had more books than most school libraries had anyway. All day long, people were coming in or being sent in from different classrooms to borrow books from Miss Daisy.

Another thing was that Miss Daisy never closed the door to her room. Even when we all left the room to go to lunch or recess, she always made sure that the door was left wide open. When we asked her about this, her answer was short and simple: "Someone might need something from our room while we are gone. We have to be sure they can get in if they need to use something that is ours."

We argued with her: "What if they take some of our stuff?"

"What if they do, if they need it? Besides, what if they are bringing something to us and the door is closed and locked? Think about all the things that we would miss if we locked people out of our lives."

It didn't make much sense to us, but she was the teacher.

When the story about Saint Valentine was over, it was time for us to make our Valentine mailboxes. Miss Daisy suggested that we wait until the next day to start them. She thought we might want to go home and find something like a shoebox as our starting place. We realized that what she had told us about leaving the door open had something to do with this. We might need big mailboxes if our door stayed open, for all the people who might want to bring us stuff.

At home that night, I hunted in the closet for the box that had come home when Daddy bought new boots at Turner's store. When I dragged the box out and announced my intention to take it to school the next day, there were plenty of questions about why the box was needed. Both my parents were accustomed to Miss Daisy's methods, but they were still curious.

I told them all about the stories of Saint Valentine, and of our curiosity about how Miss Daisy knew anything about love, seeing as how she was not married. I told them about the door of our room always being open and that this was the reason for thinking we needed bigger mailboxes this year, since anyone who wanted to could come in the door and add Valentines to our mailboxes. They listened with patient fascination.

Finally, Daddy said, "Daisy Boyd knows more than you think she knows. And she often has something up her sleeve."

I had personally never seen anything stuck up her sleeve, but I didn't want to get into this with Daddy.

The next morning, the boot box went to school with me. All of my classmates seemed to have brought boxes of some kind to start this year's mailboxes. Most of them were shoeboxes, but I did notice that Mary Caldwell had brought a Kleenex box. She would have to tear it open, I thought, to get out her Valentines.

There was no hurry in Miss Daisy's room in making the mailboxes. We could use any color from her construction paper stash that we wanted to use. She had both paste and mucilage. We even got to use her big teacher scissors with the points on the end. Years later, I knew that what we did that day had to be called "art."

Finally, Valentine's Day arrived. This year, Miss Daisy herself brought both punch and cupcakes. These were fresh and not like the ones that Eddie's mama had always brought in years past. Miss Daisy's cupcakes had big fluffs of red and white icing and little silver sprinkles on them. Some of them were even decorated with little red hearts she had cut carefully from construction paper and glued to toothpicks so they would stick up on the cupcakes.

We had cupcakes and drank good punch, and all the while Miss Daisy had us retell the stories we remembered about Saint Valentine. It was one of the best parties ever. At last, it was time for all of us to open our Valentine mailboxes. Soon, paper was flying everywhere.

For some reason, we were very quiet in announcing the numbers in Miss Daisy's class. We did count, of course, and we did tell each other how many we got. I actually was highly disappointed that I still got only twenty-eight, including the one I had given to myself. I got no Valentines at all from people outside our class who took advantage of our open door to bring them to me.

We were just about ready to start cleaning up our mess when we heard an unfamiliar sound of laughter in the back of the room. When we all turned to look, it was Willie Freedle. She had not torn into her mailbox as quickly as the rest of us. Her Valentine experience from the past did not inspire that kind of excitement. Willie was only now opening the top of her shoebox-based mailbox.

That was when her laughter started. Its sound was not familiar to us, and I later realized we had never heard Willie laugh in the four years our class had been together. She was now laughing before she touched a single Valentine, and we could see that the box was overfilled and almost pushing the lid up as she opened it.

We all watched, including a quiet Miss Daisy, as Willie opened the first Valentine. It was large and in a red envelope, the kind that Mama had told me was for people who were getting "married or something." The Valentine was from Haskel Davis, our middle-aged bachelor school janitor. No one in the world had ever gotten a Valentine from Haskel. This was the first.

The next Valentine was not as large, but it was just as impressive. It was from Mrs. Calhoun, our school lunchroom lady! She made us hot rolls every day, but we did not know she even knew about Valentine's Day.

The list went on and on. Willie got a Valentine from Mr. Stephens, the truant officer (we weren't sure we would have wanted that one), and a Valentine from Mr. Kirkpatrick, who delivered the milk and bread to school. She even got one from Mr. Bowles, the superintendent. By the time the count was all over, Willie Freedle got sixty-one Valentines in Miss Daisy's open-door fourth-grade classroom. We could not believe it. The entire room applauded Willie and cheered.

As most of us cleaned up the room, Willie and Miss Daisy were busy together. Miss Daisy had Willie choose one-third of her Valentines, and the two of them made a bulletin board using them. It stayed up long after Washington's Birthday was forgotten, showing us which holiday Miss Daisy knew was more important.

Willie took another third of her Valentines home with her. I wish I could have been there that night to hear her tell the true story of what actually did happen on that Valentine's Day in Miss Daisy Boyd's room.

The other third she kept in her desk at school. They lived there for the rest of the year. Every time Willie reached into the desk to get a pencil or some paper, we could see them. They reminded us that we still didn't know how Miss Daisy knew all about love, since she wasn't married or anything.

But maybe Daddy was right. She did know about a lot of stuff, and maybe what he meant to say was that she had *Valentines* up her sleeve.

Chapter 12

THE OCTOPUS

There was not a lot to do in Waynesville when I was a child. There were two movie theaters, a skating rink, and Charlie's Drive-In Restaurant. That was about all. This meant that anytime anything unusual came to town, it was really a big deal.

Every year or two, Rubinoff and his violin came. There were school shows and night shows. Everyone went to see Rubinoff and hoped that he would play "The Flight of the Bumblebee" as his big finale.

Every so often, Preston the Magician ("winner of the Blackstone Cup") came. He would hypnotize some volunteer teenager and have them on display on a bed in the window of Massie Furniture Company the afternoon before his big show. I remember well the year it was Grey Watkins. People gathered and gawked with amazement. That night, the show was sold out.

I once recall a tiny circus that actually set up in a field below our house. There was one small elephant and a scantily clad trick rider whom even I knew was too old to be dressed the way she was.

But of all these visiting entertainments, my perpetual favorite was simply that time each September when "the rides" came to town. Big red, black, and white posters would go up all over town: "Strates Shows—Riding Devices" were coming. Excitement was in the air!

Finally, the time would come, and Joe and I would start begging. We begged each night at the supper table. I remember that I was about eight years old and he would have been turning six when we really got interested, mostly because we heard all the other children at school talk about going to "the rides."

"Can we go to the rides? Please let us go to the rides. Don't you want to go to the rides? Everybody that we know likes to go to the rides. Will you take us to the rides? We're probably the last children in the world that haven't been to the rides. . . ." And on and on.

After spending a couple of suppertimes like that, Mama would finally give up. "Okay. Let's get it over with!" she would proclaim with a big, defeated shrug of her entire body. "But"— here came the warning—"I am going to tell you one thing right now: when we get over there, you are not going to eat *junk*. So don't even ask for it!"

As soon as the dishes were washed and dried, we all piled in our Plymouth and headed into town.

The rides were set up on part of what was normally the junior high school playground, which was also the parking lot for football games. It was the dirt field between the junior-high building and the Richesons' house. When I looked at that space years later, I could not imagine that it was big enough to hold what I clearly remember being there!

We parked the car on the side of the street next to Bill and Bert Chambers' new house. They were funny little people whom I liked. Bill always wore a little flat cap and was usually seen walking their little bowlegged bulldog.

As we were crossing the street, Mama asked the question: "Now that we are here, what do you boys want to ride first?"

At age eight, I was scared of everything, a total chicken. The only real reason I even wanted to go over there was so that I could watch and hope that someone I knew either threw up or fell out! I had no answer. Joe, however, was ready to go. I later thought that since he was only six years old, his brain had not yet come together, so he didn't know any better.

He looked at the first thing he saw. It was the gigantic circular spinning swing ride, with a ring of swings suspended by chains slinging people out from the turning centrifugal force of a huge overhead wheel. "Right there, right there, right there!" He was pointing at the swings. "I want to ride the swings and go around and around and around in the sky!"

Mama sucked wind. "No, no, no! You cannot get on that terrible, dangerous thing. We do not even know who put it together! Why, if that thing comes apart, you could fly off through the air. You could go sailing across the street and right through the front window of the Chambers' new house. You could kill their little pet bulldog right in the living room!" (I realized later that she didn't say anything about whether my brother himself might be killed.)

Before she even ended her sentence, Joe was pointing in another direction. "Right there, right there, right there! I want to ride 'The Bullet'!"

"No, no, no, no!" Mama sounded in a panic. "You cannot get on that terrible, dangerous thing! We do not even know who put it together. If that dangerous thing comes apart, you could land on the moon!"

Immediately, I thought, *Put him on there, then! Quick, put him on there now!*

By then, Joe was again off in another direction. "Right there, right there, right there! I want to ride the Ferris wheel!"

Mama could not keep up. "No, no, no, no, no! You cannot get on that terrible, dangerous thing. We do not even know who put it together. Why, if that thing comes loose, it could roll to Florida before it stops." (I thought I might get on it myself if you could be sure it would take you to Florida.)

After all of that, the only thing we actually got to ride was the merry-go-round. And we didn't get to ride on the horses either. It was obvious that they went up and down, and Mama did not know who put it together. We had to ride with her, holding her hands, on the little stupid bench that had giant ducks on each end of it.

Still, I loved the smells and sounds and sights of going to the rides.

A couple of years passed. By now, I was about ten years old and Joe was not quite eight. Summer ended, and the rides came back! We started our suppertime begging: "Can we go to the rides? You know you like to go to the rides, too. Please take us to the rides. We will *not* eat junk."

We had not yet been when, one night, Daddy looked across the table at Mama and pronounced, "Lucille, you don't even like the rides. Why don't you stay home and do something useful, and I will take the boys?"

Joe and I got into the Plymouth with Daddy. As the car rolled out of the driveway with only the three of us inside, he looked over at us and said, "Ha, ha, ha, boys. We've got it made now. We can do anything we want to do. Do you all want to eat junk?"

He parked the car, and we got out. As soon as my little brother's feet hit the ground, he started jumping up and down like a bedspring. I understood this completely, as I had seen it before. He was totally overstimulated, trying to take everything in at once.

Daddy just shook his head and said to me, "You might as well decide. Besides, you are the oldest anyway. What do you want to ride?"

The answer was both easy and clear. "The merry-go-round," was my quick reply.

We got on the merry-go-round, and for the first time in my life I got on a horse! I did not get one in the middle either. I got on a big horse right on the outside edge, where it was dangerous.

After we rode the merry-go-round three times, Daddy offered, "I've got an idea. There is a ride that wasn't here last year. Let's ride it. It's called 'The Octopus.'"

We walked over to where The Octopus had been put up. It was in the back corner of the lot, near the back of the baseball stands. As we walked up, I noticed the big sign that said, "OCTOPUS," spelled out in yellow light bulbs, about half of which were burned out. Why had this thing not been here before?

The Octopus had gigantic mechanical arms. On the end of each was what looked like a large, silvery, tubby thing. The tubby things could be opened up, and you could see that there was a little seat up in there.

When we walked up, the ride was not actually running. It was moving—lowering just one tubby thing at a time, unloading the victims from the last ride. "I'll get the tickets," Daddy said as Joe and I were hypnotized, staring at the thing. It did not look like it could go as high as either the swings or the Ferris wheel. It looked like it simply went in some version of "around." Since I was really scared of heights, this looked pretty good to me.

Daddy handed us the tickets, and Joe and I headed for the ride. We climbed up into one of the tubby things, and they closed it up and locked us in. That's when I realized my daddy had only bought two tickets. He was not coming near that thing.

Joe and I sat there laughing with anticipation of our first real ride besides the merry-go-round, while The Octopus moved only a notch at a time, so that each tubby seat was low enough to the ground for all the new passengers to be loaded. At last, it was filled.

Without any warning at all, a big greasy-looking man pulled a lever, and we took off.

It felt like the first thing that happened was that they popped your head off so that they had two parts to work with. Then The Octopus took all the heads, spun them around and around, and slung them off in one direction. At the same time, it took all the bodies, tangled them up, and spun them off in the other direction. All your internal organs were then left hanging in the middle of the air, hoping they could jump back on one end or the other as your separated parts passed back by.

Pretty soon, I had my head down between my knees with my eyes tightly closed and my little fingers in my ears so my liver couldn't squirt out through my brain. At the same time, another part of my body knew that I would never have children after this ride.

My brother, Joe, wasn't even holding on. He was waving his arms around in the air and yelling, "Whooo! This is fun! This is fun!" I knew that his brains had to be up in a tree somewhere over near the Chambers' house.

All of a sudden, he started hollering, "Look at Daddy, look at Daddy!"

I raised up and took a quick look. To my dismay, I saw my

own father standing near the ticket booth laughing his head off.

After what felt like about an hour, the thing finally stopped, but it seemed like forever before they got around to our seat to unload us. Finally, the greasy man unlocked the handles and let down the front of the seat.

Joe immediately stood up and proclaimed to the whole world, "I want to do it again."

He then started to step down from the high seat with the full belief that his foot was going to be the first thing to touch the ground. Was he ever wrong! When he stepped forward, his whole body took over its own movement. He ended up smacking full-length face first in the sawdust. It was pitiful. I knew better than to move until he recovered, or I would join him.

I watched while my brother tried to get up. He would get up on one knee, then suddenly fall over sideways. He would then try the other knee, only to fall over in the other direction. He tried to crawl along on his belly. That's when I saw the long string of green stuff coming out of his nose. It was something to watch.

Finally, he recovered.

Daddy came walking up to us and said, "Well, boys, what do you want to ride now?"

Without hesitation, Joe answered, "The merry-go-round."

We got on, but this time neither one of us climbed on a horse. No, we stayed seated safely on the little bench with the ducks on the end.

In a few more days, this year's time of the rides came to an end. They were taken apart and loaded on trucks so they could be hauled to some other little town where the people had nothing better to do. We thought the ride business to be all over until the next year . . . we thought!

Sometime after that, our family was all at home together on

a Sunday afternoon. We heard the kitchen door open, and suddenly my aunt Eddie stuck her head around the corner into the living room.

Aunt Eddie was our mother's little sister. She lived fairly close to us and was often coming over to our house. Usually, she came with her whole family: Uncle David and our cousins, Kay and Andy. But today, she had come on her own.

"Come in, Eddie," Mama invited. "What's going on today?"

With a sheepish smile, Aunt Eddie reached behind her and held up a basket. We went to look at the same time we heard the mewing sound. In the basket were two kittens.

My mother spent her childhood growing up on a farm. She was so glad to get away from that farm when she grew up and became a schoolteacher. She was finished with all animals. We did not have pets of any kind at our house. Mother's proclamation was that she was not going to feed an animal that did not work. She did not like dogs. I actually thought she was afraid of them. She really did not like cats.

"Cats are nasty," she would argue. "Just imagine something that digs its own bathroom with its own hands! Cats jump up on your lap without an invitation. Then they lick your face. And if they smell milk on your breath, they will lick you right on the lips. Then they jump down and slime around your legs. I can't stand that!"

I would argue back, "Cats are not slimy. They are furry."

Mother would not lose the argument. "It's their attitude!" she concluded.

Joe and I knew that she was not happy with Aunt Eddie bringing these cats into our house.

"What in the world are you doing with these cats?" she asked her sister.

"Aren't they cute? I got them from Mrs. Galloway as presents for Kay's birthday."

Suddenly, I understood everything. Kay was, of course, my cousin. I knew exactly when her birthday was, and it was not her birthday. No, Kay's birthday was not going to come around for two more weeks.

Suddenly, all of us understood why Aunt Eddie had come over with the cats. She wanted us to keep them for her until time for Kay's birthday—to hide the cats for two weeks.

Mama had two words to say about that idea: "*En . . . oh!* Not in this house!"

Aunt Eddie looked shocked. "What am I going to do, then? I was counting on your help. I don't know what to do."

Suddenly, my brother, Joe, piped up. "I'll do it!" he offered with excitement. "I would like to do it!"

"How are you going to take care of these cats if they cannot come in the house?" Mama countered.

"I'll keep them in the garage," was Joe's answer.

"They're nasty." Mama wouldn't give up.

"I'll wash my hands every time I touch them." Joe wouldn't give up either.

"They'll still be nasty," she kept on.

"I'll wash my hands every time I look at them."

"They'll still be nasty."

"I'll wash my hands every time I think about them." Joe just kept on!

Aunt Eddie joined the argument: "It's only two weeks, and I even brought the food!" She held up a paper bag, obviously full.

"I give up!" Mama folded. "Okay, you can keep them two weeks, under one condition." She pointed her finger at Joe as she laid out the limits. "You cannot give them names. If you give them names, you know what is going to happen. You will get attached to them, they will get attached to you, everyone will think they live here, and we will never get rid of them."

Joe's face fell. But he finally agreed: "Okay, no names. I'll just have to call them 'Right' and 'Left.'"

Everyone laughed except Mama.

So the plan was made. Joe kept the cats in the garage behind the house and fed them there morning and night. He washed his hands about two hundred times each day. He was totally happy.

The next morning, Joe came back into the house after feeding the kittens. "Do we have any more baskets?" he asked Mama.

"What do you need with more baskets? What's wrong with that one?" she wondered.

"Those cats are just like us. They won't quit fighting. I need to separate them."

There was a little room on the back of our house that everyone called "that room." In "that room," we kept everything that no one on the face of the earth would ever again need in their life . . . but they might. It contained every flattened brown paper grocery bag that had ever come into our house from the grocery store, deflated footballs and basketballs that would never hold air again, small kidney-shaped pans for every time someone in our family had been in the hospital, every piece of Tupperware ever made that had a lost lid, Christmas-tree lights that didn't work last year but might somehow come back on next year . . . and an assortment of old Easter baskets.

Mama headed out there and soon came back with two Easter baskets. They were just alike and even still had faded pink plastic grassy stuff in the bottom. She gave the baskets to Joe, he separated the cats and put one into each basket, and the whole world was happy.

The following day was a Saturday, so our whole family was at home. After lunch, Joe headed out to the garage to check on the cats. He was not gone five minutes when we heard screaming.

It was Joe, screaming his head off. The sound was not coming from the direction of the garage, though. It was coming from the backyard of our house. As he kept screaming, you could tell that he was coming toward the house. He was yelling words, but he was shrieking so desperately that his voice seemed to turn wrong side out, and we could not understand a word he said.

He got to the door, and it flew open. Joe came crying into the house, and the first words we could understand were, "They're *dead*, they're *dead*, they're *dead*, *dead*, *dead*!"

Our entire family was running toward the door, heading out into the yard to see what in the world had happened.

When we arrived in the yard, there they were: the two little cats, flat on the ground. You could tell that they were breathing, but not very successfully. They were almost coughing and wheezing.

One of them tried to get up off of the ground, and it fell right over on its side, legs trying to walk in thin air. The other one tried to get up, and it fell the same way. Then they began to try to crawl along the ground on their bellies, and we saw long, slimy, green stuff coming out of their noses.

"They're not dead!" Daddy announced. "But what in this world happened to them?"

We were looking at Joe. He picked up the two baskets, one in each hand, and as he swung them around and around over his head, he answered, "I let them ride The Octopus!" Then he disintegrated into tears. "I'm *sorry*! They didn't do any better than we did."

Mama walked over to the two little cats. She looked down

at them, then did something that none of us believed. With her own two little cat-hating hands, she reached down and picked up the cats. She held the cats up against her heart like she loved them. Mama began petting the little cats until in no time they were purring happily.

And she gave them names—or at least we thought she did. As she keep petting and they kept purring, she called one of them "Pitiful" and the other one "Unfortunate." Then she announced, "I better take them in the house."

We all watched, still in disbelief, as Mama took the cats into the house where we lived! Not only that, she took them right into the kitchen where we ate food. And while she kept holding and petting them, she got hold of the telephone and called Aunt Eddie.

We were all listening. "Eddie," we heard her start softly, "I hate to have to call to tell you this. There is a problem. I hate to be the one to tell you this, but you are going to have to get Kay some more cats for her birthday . . . because *I love these*, and we are going to keep them."

And for the rest of her life, every time you went to see my mama, you had to put up with: jumping on your lap, licking your face, rubbing around your legs—Pitiful and Unfortunate, my mama's first cats.

Chapter 13

NOTHING WORKS
BUT HER MOUTH

Mama did not teach school during the years between the time when she and Daddy got married and the year when Joe and I were both safely in school. Then, that year, when I was in the second grade and he was in church-basement kindergarten, she decided to go back to resume the career she was to practice for thirty-eight more years.

She had needed no special help with the two of us during the seven-plus years when she was mothering full-time at home. However, when she again started teaching school, there were times when we all needed the help of a babysitter so that Mama could work through the tasks and errands that were not possible with two small boys as her helpers.

The solution was near at hand. Just up Plott Creek Road and over the hill from our house lived Miss Annie McIntosh, an older lady whom Mama and Daddy both knew well because in those days everybody knew everybody. Miss Annie was a widow whose four sons and one daughter were grown, who could be recruited to be the called-in babysitter whenever we needed one.

Miss Annie drove an old, gray 1939 Chevrolet she called "Rattling Rachel." She would drive herself to our house to keep us whenever Mama called her. Miss Annie would come creeping down the dirt road, peering through the steering wheel of the Chevy as she drove. She would pull into our driveway, get out of the car, and always without knocking come right in the house.

She carried a gigantic fake-leather pocketbook with double handles. As she sat down in a chair, she would plop the big pocketbook on the floor beside her. All on its own, it would pop open, and a whole raft of old, fluffy Kleenex tissues would float out and land all around it. There were unknown other dangers hiding beneath the remaining tissues.

After a few moments of recovery from the one-mile drive, Miss Annie would get up and wander around the house gathering up all the scattered books we had left here and there and everywhere. Then she would return to the Kleenex-guarded chair and utter totally predictable words: "Do you boys want me to read you a little story?" We almost always did.

Sometimes when Mama called for Miss Annie's help, she could not come. On most of those days, she would say, "Bring them up here. I can't leave the house right now, but they can stay here with me just fine."

My brother and I loved those days. Miss Annie lived in a big, old, rambling house with a basement, a first floor with a wide porch running more than halfway around, an assortment of bedrooms on the second floor, and even a walk-up attic over that. It was a warren of treasures, turns, and hiding places.

Being an old lady, Miss Annie took a lot of naps. As soon as she was asleep, Joe and I would engage in a quiet session of our favorite hobby: snooping and prowling. We snooped and prowled so much that we knew not only what was in every room on every floor, we knew exactly what was in every closet and every drawer in every room on every floor. We were championship snoopers and prowlers.

Of all the curious places at Miss Annie's house, one of the most fascinating was what she called "my garage apartment." The garage apartment looked very much like a miniature version of her house. It formed the second story of the garage in which the old Chevy lived, and we watched an interesting parade of people move in and out of the apartment throughout our childhood snooping years. Joe and I spied on all of them.

We could sit in the garage, hiding behind the Chevy, and listen for water to come down the big black drainpipe, knowing for certain that when we heard water, someone had just been to the bathroom upstairs. We would climb up into a large red maple tree in the side yard and pretend to one another that we could see into the apartment windows, even though both of us knew very well that we could not. We would even graphically tell one another about what we pretended that we were seeing.

For a short while, an older man named Arthur lived there. Arthur drove a little red Studebaker of a 1950-ish vintage. It looked to us like a small airplane without wings. Arthur had even made a small silver propeller and attached it to the nose of the Studebaker. As the Studebaker rolled along, the little propeller spun wildly. Arthur told Daddy that the propeller made the Studebaker get better gasoline mileage. Daddy told Mama that if the Studebaker got good gas mileage, it was because it saved on gas by sucking the fumes off all the liquor Arthur had been drinking.

We were told that Arthur had formerly lived with his wife but that one day she went to the store to get some bread and forgot the way back home. This meant that Arthur no longer needed a whole house, and the apartment was just right for him. In spite of the assertions that the apartment was "just right," Arthur did not live there very long.

After he moved on, the apartment was occupied by Mrs. Fox and Mrs. Way. They were old ladies who drove an ancient La-Salle. The LaSalle was chocolate brown with cream-colored fenders and was very elegant, though old. It was so long that they had to maneuver it back and forth over and over again to get it turned around in the small driveway.

We learned that Mrs. Fox was Mrs. Way's mother, though they both seemed so old to us that we couldn't make much helpful sense out of that knowledge. Mrs. Fox always dressed for church, wearing an old fur piece that looked like a troop of little dead foxes hanging around her neck. They had eyes and teeth and tails, and I told my brother that they would bite you if you got close to them.

The most wonderful thing was that they were church-hoppers. This meant that about once a month, they came to the Methodist church. Since we sat near the front and one of the only empty pews was right in front of us, when they came to our church they would end up sitting there. All through the church service, the dead foxes dangled over the back of their pew and right in front of us. They terrified my brother and kept me from getting bored with the sermon.

I knew that these dead ornaments were the very reason that Mrs. Fox was so named. Mrs. Way's name I understood also. Not yet knowing all the vagaries of English spelling, I clearly understood Mrs. Way's name when Daddy observed that she was "a right fleshy woman."

When Joe and I were in the six- to eight-year-old range, a new tenant moved into the garage apartment. His name was Robert

Louis Fitzgerald, and he was a new policeman in town. We came to like Robert Louis Fitzgerald very much, and he, being unmarried and without children, became almost our playmate.

When it was his turn to be on call, he drove a police car home at night. It was one of only two police cars in town and had to be ready if needed. The car he always got to bring was a 1953 Plymouth that was painted black and white and had a single red light that could blink slowly just above the center of the windshield. One day, Daddy looked at the car and said, "That's not a police car, that's a joke. Why, that six-cylinder Plymouth couldn't pull a wet booger out of a baby's nose!" Mama turned red and frowned, but Robert Louis Fitzgerald agreed.

The police car was the real reason for two little boys' friendship with the policeman. Robert Louis Fitzgerald would invite the two of us to play in the police car and check out all of the switches and buttons, just to see what they would do.

There was one switch that made the red light on top of the car come on and start blinking. There was a button that you could press and it would make the siren wail unbrokenly as long as you held it. When you released the button, the siren would start to wind down, and the best sounds were made by pushing it in and out and in and out over and over again.

The police car had two exterior spotlights that were mounted on either side of the windshield. When it was dark, Robert Louis Fitzgerald showed Joe and me how to turn on the spotlights and work the controls from inside the car. We had sword fights in the dark with the light beams. We even learned how to talk through the radio with the dial set to the right place to make our voices come out through the front of the grille of the car.

Robert Louis Fitzgerald would come driving home in the car in the afternoon. He would get out and would be wearing his black policeman's uniform, complete with his wide black belt and his pistol at his side. The black belt had little leather loops that held a row of bullets running all the way around the back. It looked so exciting and so dangerous.

He would take out a bullet and show it to us. Then he would say, "Do y'all want to touch a bullet?"

"What will it do?" my brother would innocently ask.

I gave the answer myself: "If you touch it and your fingernail happens to accidentally hit the bullet, it will go off and kill you!"

We would stand way back and barely touch the bullets with great fear and trembling.

One day, an old stray dog wandered out of the woods and into Miss Annie's yard. Miss Annie saw the old dog staggering and slobbering and called us inside. "That may be a mad dog!" she said. She called Robert Louis Fitzgerald at the police station and asked if he would come home quickly and shoot the dog.

Soon, the police car came in the driveway.

My brother, Joe, and I wanted to watch. We had never seen anyone shoot a dog. Miss Annie would not let us watch. We did, however, listen to everything. We heard the gun go, *Bang, bang!*

"Why did he have to shoot two times?" I asked Miss Annie.

"Well," she mused, "he is either a bad shot or he killed real good!"

By the time I was about nine years old, Robert Louis Fitzgerald moved out of the garage apartment. He told us that he was getting married and that he and his wife-to-be were buying a house in town. The police car was gone. A lot of our fun was over.

Joe and I got older. Miss Annie got older. By the time Joe was eight and I was ten, she had to be at least eighty years old.

Then another thing happened: as we all got older, Joe and I decided that we did not need a babysitter anymore. "We are too old to keep having that old lady watch everything we do," we both protested to Mama.

Daddy tried to reason with us. "Don't think of Miss Annie as a babysitter," he started. "Think of her as a wise old teacher. She is an old, old lady. That means that she has seen a lot of life and has had a lot of experience. She knows how to handle things that I do not even know how to handle because I have not lived as long as she has. If you'll watch her and talk with her and listen to her, she could really teach you a lot. She is a wise old woman."

Joe and I were not at all impressed. The only word of all those Daddy had used that we even heard was *old*, and we did not want to keep having her as our babysitter, no matter what you called it. There seemed no escape.

When I was twelve years old and Joe was almost ten, we moved to the new house. At the new house, we got our first television set. "Now, we will not need a babysitter," Joe said. "We have a television set. How could we possibly manage to watch two things at once? We need to get rid of that babysitter." With this, Joe and I both thought that we had seen the last of Miss Annie for sure.

One day not long after we were well settled in the new house, Mama came in to where Joe and I were playing. "Boys," she started, "tonight your daddy and I are going over to John and Roselle Nesbit's house for supper. We are going to stay over there for a while and play bridge with some other friends who are coming. You boys know most of them. I have called Miss Annie, and she is going to come over here and be your babysitter."

"We don't need her," my little brother insisted.

"Why not?" Mama smiled at him.

"We have told you before. We are too old for a babysitter. Besides, we have a television set. How could we watch a television set and a babysitter at the same time? We already told you that. Didn't you listen?"

Joe should have stopped talking right then and there, but his nine-year-old mouth just kept running: "That old lady is no good as a babysitter anyway. She is so old that she can't even make us behave. I can outrun her. . . ." He kept on talking while Mama just watched and gave him more rope. "That old lady is so old that nothing on her works but her mouth. She can't do anything."

Mama did not even bother to argue with him. She simply said, "We'll see." I noticed that she was smiling.

Later in the afternoon, Mama called us to come to the kitchen and eat our supper before she and Daddy went out for the evening. Joe and I ate while the two of them finished getting ready to go. Pretty soon, we heard a car come into the driveway. When we looked out the window, it was Miss Annie's old gray Chevrolet. We watched with dismay as she got out of the car.

She came in the door as Mama and Daddy were pulling on their coats to leave. As they left, I heard Daddy say, "Try to learn something from Miss Annie while she's here, boys." And they were gone.

Miss Annie came into the new living room and dropped her giant pocketbook on the floor beside the recliner chair where Daddy usually sat. When the pocketbook hit the floor, the top popped open and about a dozen Kleenex tissues floated up into the air and then settled on the floor all around it. As they settled, Miss Annie settled into the big chair. "Well, boys, I am glad to see both of you. Do you want me to read you a little story before it's time for you to go to bed?"

Joe answered, "No. We are too old for stories. Stories are for babies. We want to watch television."

"Okay," she easily agreed, "we will all watch television."

I walked across the room and turned on the new RCA television set. We only got one channel. Joe and I sat down to watch Channel 13, Asheville, North Carolina, with Miss Annie tuned in beside us.

When we had moved to the new house, Daddy and Mama

had bought some new furniture to fill up the spaces in this house that was bigger than our old house on Plott Creek Road. The biggest purchase was a gigantic 1955 aquamarine-colored sectional sofa. The sofa ran down one wall on the side of the living room, turned the corner, and continued across the back. It was upholstered in loopy nylon stuff that you could easily get most anything caught in if you were not careful. The sofa was so long that Joe and I could get on opposite ends and we were so far apart that we did not even have to touch one another. We loved it.

The program that came on Channel 13 was a special feature show about the circus. As we started watching, trapeze artists came into view. They started swinging above the center ring of the circus, flipping through the air and catching one another at the end of each flight. "I wish we could do that!" Joe excitedly addressed the television set.

When the trapeze act was over, the tightrope walkers came out. As we all watched them balance their way across the high wire, Joe offered again, "I wish we could do that!" He was so excited.

In a few minutes, that act was over and a troupe of acrobats came across the television screen. We watched them run into the circus ring and begin to turn flips as they ran. "We can do that!" Joe was so ecstatic that he jumped out of his seat with excitement.

He and I took one of the cushions from the big sofa and put it in the floor in the center of the living room. Once it was carefully placed, we would run across the room, jump on the cushion, and flip in the air, using our hands for leverage. Every time we did a couple of flips, we would look back at the television set to get more ideas. Every time the acrobats did something more complex, Joe assured all of us, "We can do that, too!" Miss Annie simply sat there and watched the whole thing.

In no time, we had removed all five cushions from the big sofa, including the curved one from the corner section. They were aligned in a row across the living room. Joe and I were now going way down the hall so that we had enough distance to get a good running start before we jumped onto the first cushion. We were so clever.

My ten-year-old brother came running full speed down the hall. He jumped on the first pillow, then landed on his hands on the middle pillow, and when his feet went up in the air, his hands slipped and he fell over sideways. Joe's feet hit the coffee table, and Mama's brand-new floor lamp flopped over against the wall, but it did not break!

Miss Annie stood up from the rocking chair in which she was sitting. "Boys," she announced in a steady voice, "that is about enough circus for tonight. It is now time for you to go to bed."

At that, little brother Joe looked at the eighty-some-year-old woman, cocked his hip to the side, stuck out his tongue, and went, "*Pffffffttttttttttttt!*" with spit flying out of his mouth at the same time.

Miss Annie did not say a word. She simply reached down and poked all of the escaped Kleenex tissues back into her big pocket-book, picked up the now-closed handbag, walked out the door of our house, got into her gray Chevrolet, and drove away.

Joe and I danced around the living room, laughing and cele-brating. "We did it! We got rid of the babysitter!" We were almost singing the refrain over and over to one another. The two of us thought somehow that we had seen the end of Miss Annie.

With our babysitting watchdog now safely out of sight, my brother and I proceeded to turn the house into the circus. We turned Daddy's big chair upside down. Then we would run up the back of the overturned chair and flip in the air off the other side. We climbed on top of the dining-room table and pretended that the crack where you pulled it apart in the middle was the tightwire line. Then we walked, pretending great skill at balancing, back and forth along the crack.

After that, we took the fallen floor lamp and laid it across two chairs to make a sort-of hurdle out of it. We would run and jump over the hurdle one time, then run and slide under it the next.

The great climax came when Joe went over to the living-room curtains and caught hold of the bottom end of one of them. "I'm going to climb up these curtains and swing across the room," he announced.

At that very moment, our front doorbell rang. Joe went running across the room to see who could possibly be at the door. I went to look out the front window to see if I could tell who might be there.

There, parked in the driveway in front of our house, was a black-and-white Plymouth police car. It sat idling with the motor running, with the red light slowly blinking on the roof. My brother opened the door. There, in his full uniform, stood Robert Louis Fitzgerald with his gun drawn.

"What do you want?" Joe nearly whispered.

"Where are your parents?" came the policeman's quick reply.

I tried to intervene. "Why do you need them?" was my question.

Robert Louis Fitzgerald made a chortling sound. "Why do I need them? I'll tell you why I need them. We just had an emergency telephone call at the police station. An anonymous person called to report that someone was wrecking the Davis house. Do you boys know anything about that?"

My ten-year-old brother was trying to act bold. He was trying to use his little body to block the policeman's view into our house. At the same time, I was desperately trying to right things in the living room into some sort of reasonable order. Neither of us was successful.

In what seemed like less than a moment, the policeman we thought was our friend was standing in the middle of our wrecked living room. He did not look friendly. He used his still-drawn pistol as a pointer as he looked around the room and observed, "My goodness! What in this world got into this place? It's either wild animals or hardened criminals that could have done this. Where are your parents?" He looked sharply at both of us.

I asked the question again: "Why do you need to know where they are?"

"Because"—his voice had a deep and serious tone—"I have to arrest them and put both of them in jail."

"What for? They didn't do anything?" Joe was almost crying now.

"That's just the problem. They didn't do what they were supposed to do. When parents go out, they are supposed to leave a babysitter with their children. They obviously did not do that. I can't figure out how all this destruction happened, but if there had been a responsible babysitter here with you, none of it could possibly have happened.

"It is against all laws to leave children unattended at home. Look here." He held up two pairs of shiny handcuffs. "I have two pairs of strong handcuffs—a pair for each one of them. You boys better tell me where they are. They are liable to be in jail a long time for a crime like this."

My little brother was wailing, "Dooooon't put my mama in jail! She doesn't know what to do in jail. I don't know about my daddy."

Robert Louis Fitzgerald had a very studied and serious look

on his face. He slowly offered, "Well, boys, if you had someone here taking care of you, I would not have to arrest your parents. But you don't, so I guess I will have to do it. Unless one of you has a better idea."

That was all it took. Joe raised his hand like he was in school, but he was already talking: "I have a great idea. I really do like it a lot when Miss Annie McIntosh is our babysitter. She is good at it. Is there any way to find out if she can come and help us straighten everything out?"

"That might work." There was the hint of a grin on the policeman's face. "Let me use your telephone to call her and see if she is at home right now." He disappeared into the kitchen.

By the time he came back out, Miss Annie's old gray car was pulling up into our driveway, and Joe and I had the living room put back together better than ever.

Robert Louis Fitzgerald told us to have a good evening, and as he went out the door to get into the police car and leave, Miss Annie came back into the house.

She dropped the pocketbook, and the same old Kleenex tissues jumped out as it popped open. She herself dropped into the now-righted easy chair. "Well, boys, do you want to watch some more television?"

I did not say a word. Somehow, I knew that my brother would handle everything.

Sure enough, he did. "No," he said. "We got tired while you were gone. We were straightening up the house so Mama and Daddy will be proud of us when they get home. We are tired. Could we go on to bed now . . . and would you read us a little story?"

"If that is what you boys really want," the old lady smiled, "you know that I would."

We went into our bedroom and got into our twin beds. Miss Annie pulled a chair up between the two beds and read us some kind of story. I had no idea in this world what the story was about. There was no way I could pay attention to what she was reading. My entire mind was occupied with images of our mama and daddy going to jail in handcuffs. It had been a close call.

Finally, our parents came home from their evening at the Nesbits'. Joe and I were still awake when they came in and thankfully saw Miss Annie out the door to go home for the second time that night.

When Mama came in to check on us, she could tell that we were not asleep. She didn't turn on the light but looked down at us in the darkness of the room. "We're home, boys. How did you get along with Miss Annie?"

I was not inclined to share my opinions of the evening with anyone, but Joe was. "We got along just fine!" he said.

Mama asked, "Did you watch television?"

"Not much," Joe answered a little too quickly. "It wasn't any good. There was nothing on but an old circus show, and they didn't do anything interesting at all. Besides, we were tired. We asked to go to bed. Miss Annie read us a good story. We asked for that, too." He rested his case.

"That's nice," Mama answered as Daddy joined her, listening in the soft darkness. "What was the story about?"

Personally, I had no idea what the story had been about, but Joe had a summary ready: "It was about two little boys. They almost got in trouble . . . but not quite!"

"That sounds like a good story," Mama mused. "I'll have to thank her for reading that to you."

Now, it was Daddy's turn to talk. "I told you that you boys would always have a good time with Miss Annie. You may not need an actual babysitter, but that old lady has had so much experience in her life that you can't keep from learning things just by being around her."

And he was right. We did not know it at the time, but as it turned out, Miss Annie ended up being our babysitter until my brother and I both graduated from high school.

We also learned an important personal lesson at a fortunate early age: if you are messing with an old lady, it does not matter if the only thing that works is her mouth, you are going to be the loser. So you might as well give up from the start.

Chapter 14

BROKEN BONES

Mama was the oldest of the nine children in her family. There were seven girls in a row, then two little brothers. The earliest memories of her life were of taking care of children. Her youngest brother was born when she was a sophomore in college.

After practicing on her own little brothers and sisters, when Joe and I came along, she was sure that she was going to "get it right" as a parent. We were going to be the perfect children. Whenever we were at home with her, Mama seemed to have one main thing to say about most everything we did: "Don't do that!" It was her parenting motto.

Instead of learning "Don't do that," what I really learned was how important it was to spend time at my grandmother's house. She had a different motto. No matter what we did there, her main thing to say was, "You are so cute!" I loved spending time at my grandmother's house.

One day, we were at Grandmother's and Joe and I did something that did not please Mama. We were not surprised to hear the words, "Boys, don't do that!"

Grandmother took up for us. "Why are you being so hard on those cute boys?" was her question.

"Well," Mama took up for herself, "I certainly wouldn't have done something like they did when I was their age."

"You're right about that," Grandmother smiled. "You were worse!"

Then she turned to us. "Come here, boys. Do you want to hear a story about when your mother was a little girl?"

Of course we did. Mama moved to the far side of the room. She wanted to pretend that she was not interested in the story but at the same time wanted to be sure that she could hear everything that was going on.

Grandmother then told us the story. Mama was about seven years old when it all happened. At that time, all of the farm work was done with a team of oxen. One day, her father, my granddaddy, went off somewhere for the day. He was gone all day.

When he came home late that afternoon, he called all of the family together and told them, "I bought something today. Everybody come out on the porch and see what I got."

The family followed him to the porch. He lined them up where they could all see, then pointed out across the yard to the trees at the edge of the garden. "See that thing standing there? That is called a 'horse.' It is going to do the work that the oxen have been doing, but it is a lot faster and easier to handle. Now, listen, it is not a toy! It is a workhorse only. Whatever you do, do not try to ride on it."

At age seven, that was all Mama needed to hear. She knew that she had to ride that horse or she would die. That was all there was to it. She knew that she had to watch and wait for a time when no one was looking. So she waited.

One day, no one was around the house but her. She slipped

out to the back of the barn, where the horse was tied. It looked tame and peaceful. This would be easy. There was only one prob-lem: she was short and the horse was tall. How would she get up on top of the horse? Then she saw the solution. Right beside where the horse was tied, there was a gate that opened into the back of the barn. It was made of long slats and looked remarkably like a ladder.

So she opened the gate until it was right beside the horse. Then she climbed to the top of the gate, stood on the very top, and jumped onto the horse's back. The horse did not calmly stand there. No, it took a big jump and tossed her right off on the ground on the other side.

She landed on her right arm. As soon as she landed, she knew that something was wrong. Her arm did not look straight the way it had all of her life. Then the pain hit, and she realized what had happened. Her right arm was broken, both bones, halfway be-tween her wrist and her elbow. She went crying, almost carrying her arm with her left hand, back to the house.

Then the real trouble started. Where they lived, back there on the farm, it was about sixteen miles to town. They never went to town at all. There was no way to get there. And if they did some-how get to town, they did not even know a doctor.

But right up the road lived Uncle Will. He knew all about herbs, and so he would have to do. He was brought down to the house and declared that he could set a broken bone "as well as the next man."

Uncle Will walked out to the little creek below the garden and cut a short limb from a willow tree. He skinned all of the bark off of the limb with his pocketknife and split the limb right down the middle. Then he smoothed both sides with his little knife.

When all was ready, he and Granddaddy put Mama in a chair

at the kitchen table with her broken arm laid out on the table. Granddaddy held Mama so that she couldn't jump or jerk. Uncle Will, on the other side of the table, got hold of her by the wrist. Suddenly, he *pulled* her arm straight out as hard as he could, and while it was pulled he told Grandmother how to wrap the splints to either side of the now-straight broken arm. That is how it healed.

When Joe and I heard that, we looked over at Mama. She was listening with her head down in her folded arms.

Joe asked her, "Mama, did that hurt?"

She raised her head. "I cannot tell you. I passed out. But if I had not passed out, there are still no words I could use with children to tell you how much it hurt."

The broken arm happened in the late winter, as that was when Granddaddy had bought the horse so it would be ready for work in the spring. Now that she was set and splinted up, Mama hoped that the arm would be well by Easter. Her mother, my grandmother, had made her a new Easter dress, and she wanted to be able to wear it. The Easter dress had sleeves that were like big puffs at the top and were very close-fitted with tiny buttons from the elbow to the wrist. Until the splints came off, there would be no way to wear the new dress.

Every day or two, Mama would walk up to Uncle Will's house so he could feel of her arm and give her a guess about when it might be well. He wouldn't dare let her take off the splints until long after there was no pain when he felt her arm.

Finally, that time came. It was the week before Easter, just in time for her to get into the new dress.

On Easter morning, Mama was up before anyone else in the house. She was happily dressed and ready to go before anyone else was out of bed.

When Grandmother got up and saw her, she asked, "What

are you doing up when it is not even daylight yet?"

"I am ready to go to church so people can look at me!" Mama proudly (and honestly) answered her mother.

"Well, we are not ready. I have to fix breakfast and get all of the little children ready. It looks like you're not going to be much help to me, since you are already dressed up in your new outfit. At least you can stay out of the way. Why don't you go outside and look over there next to the garden where all those daffodils are blooming and pick us a big bunch of flowers? Get us two bunches—one to take to church and one to go on the table for dinner when we get back. Don't get dirty."

Mama headed out the door in the fresh, early light. She walked over and began to look at the daffodils. All of a sudden, she heard a neighing sound. When she looked up, there was the horse. It was tied right beside the gate where Granddaddy almost always seemed to keep it.

I know how to do it now, she thought. She had spent a lot of time thinking about it.

Mama forgot all about daffodils. She hiked herself around the side of the barn and patted the horse on the neck. Then she opened the big gate until it looked like a ladder beside the big horse. In her new Easter dress, she climbed to the top of the ladder.

Mama later admitted that she had seen pictures in a book of women riding sidesaddle, and that is what gave her the idea about how to handle the dress. She jumped backwards from the top of the gate and landed on the horse with both legs on the same side.

The big workhorse jerked wildly. Mama went head over heels off the opposite side. This time, she landed with an audible cracking noise—it was her *left* arm this time. It was broken in almost exactly the same place as the just-healed right arm.

With no daffodils, she walked, crying, back to the house.

Grandmother just shook her head. "Law, law," she moaned. "You just keep walking right on up there to Uncle Will's house. I'll send your daddy to help."

The new dress was ruined, as the two men had to cut her out of the left-arm sleeve. Uncle Will still had the splints. The only difference this time was that they were seated at Uncle Will's kitchen table. Granddaddy held her, Uncle Will pulled her arm, and the splints found a new home! She passed out just like the time before.

Mama was looking out the window like she was not listening at all as Grandmother finished the story. It was like she was trying to pretend that she wasn't there and that she didn't know anything at all about the story that was being told.

It was not over yet. Grandmother looked at Joe and me. "You see, boys," she smiled. "You boys did not invent evil. It is an inherited trait. You got it from your mother! Go over there and feel of her arms."

Mama could not escape. Joe and I went over to where she was seated. She had to cooperate. We each felt one forearm, then the other. About halfway between the elbow and wrist on each arm, we could feel a big lump on the bone. This was the thickened bulge where the breaks had healed.

We loved that story when we first heard it. It was later, however, when its full meaning came through to our whole family.

Up until I was twelve years old, we lived at our "old house" on Plott Creek Road. There were no children our age anywhere within playing distance. Joe and I were stuck having to play with one another. We had no idea what it would be like to have playmate neighbors. It was simply not part of our world.

At the end of my sixth-grade year, the whole world changed. After looking and saving for years, our family moved to the "new house." It was big (to us) and had a wonderful large and flat front yard. We also had playmates.

The house straight behind us, only across Daddy's new garden from our house, was the Leatherwoods' house. Mr. Leatherwood, our first elementary-school principal, was now the school superintendent. Mrs. Leatherwood taught at the high school. We went to the same church, and they had been good friends of my parents for years.

The Leatherwoods also had two children. Larry was the older, and he was almost the same age that I was. His little brother, Ronnie, was the same age as my little brother, Joe. We had something we had never had in our lives: playmates right through our back fence.

Every day, we would come home from school and go over to Larry and Ronnie's house. We would get something to eat. Then they would come with us back over to our house. We would get something to eat.

Pretty soon, it would be Larry who made the suggestion: "Want to play football?"

We loved to play football. The front yard of our new house was long and wide and totally flat. It was surrounded by an edging of white pine trees that defined the playing area perfectly. No one could have planned a better football field for four kids.

Larry, Ronnie, Joe, and I would grab the football and head out into the yard.

"Are you boys going to play football?" Mama would ask as we headed out the door. "You boys better not get hurt. I want you to be sure you play *touch* football so you won't get hurt!"

We would laugh. We thought that was a silly request. After all, how could you possibly tackle someone without touching them? We laughed again.

As soon as the four of us got out in the yard each day, the first thing was to choose up teams. It always came out the same way: big boys against the little boys. Larry and I told Joe and Ronnie that it was not fair for brothers to be on the same team, and they never did seem to figure out that there was any other way to do it. We always kicked off to them first. Somehow, it made them think they had a real advantage.

There was only one problem with football in the yard. It was called "the big picture window." Right in the center of the house, right where the imaginary goalposts would be, there was a gigantic floor-to-ceiling picture window. We lived in fear of breaking it.

Mama would actually go in the living room and talk to the window when we went out for our football games. She would look at it sadly and intone, "You're going to get broken. I just know you're going to get broken."

One Saturday, we were playing football in the yard when Daddy was at home. He watched us for a few minutes and seemed to be thinking about what he was seeing.

When we took our next break, he called us over to the side to talk with us. "Come over here, boys. I want to tell you something. We have some new rules here about football. Let me explain this to you. This is a single-ended football field," he started.

"What does that mean?" It was Joe who asked.

"That means that it doesn't have two ends. It only has one end, and"—he was pointing away from the house—"both ends are down there! No matter who has the ball, you need to run that way, away from the house.

"Now, listen to this: no more kicking toward the window, no throwing toward the window, no running toward the window, no looking toward the window, no thinking about the window. No matter what, boys, go *that* way." He again pointed away from the house.

We had the most mixed-up football games anyone could ever have had in this world. First of all, we had to kick off aiming away from the house. Then, when the others got the ball, they had to turn around and keep running away from the house. It made no sense, except that no one could ever catch the kicked ball anyway, so it would bounce on the ground, then we would get it, turn around, and start over in the other direction.

One day, Larry and I were kicking off to Joe and Ronnie. I held the ball while Larry ran and kicked. The ball went tumbling end over end toward my brother, Joe. I knew that Joe was ten years old and had not caught a football in more than twenty-five years. But on this day, the ball simply fell into his arms. He had no choice. The ball caught itself.

Joe stood there not knowing what to do. Instead of blocking for him, Ronnie turned around and started running in the other direction. Larry and I had no choice at all; we jumped on Joe and both tackled him to the ground, hard.

When we got off and Joe tried to get up, he was crying. He was also very funny looking. One of his arms looked completely normal. The other arm was limply hanging longer and lower than it was supposed to. We had broken his right collarbone snap in two.

We called for Mama. She came out and immediately put Joe and me into the car and sent Larry and Ronnie running home. We headed for the emergency room at the Haywood County Hospital.

I still do not know what doctor was on duty. It does not matter. Joe came out of the emergency room with a figure-eight-shaped strapping bandage that pulled his shoulders way back to hold the broken bone where it could heal. It must have been horribly painful.

When we got back to the house, Larry and Ronnie came over

to see what had happened at the hospital. As soon as all three of us looked at Joe, Larry and I jointly began to call him "Chicken Boy." He really did look like a big old chicken with his shoulders pulled so far back.

We would imitate sounds: "*Pwwwaaakkk, pwak, pwak, pwak.* Look at Chicken Boy. Going to lay an egg?"

Joe was furious, but he was in so much pain that he could not do anything about it.

The collarbone was broken in the late winter. Now that Joe was tied back together, he began to hope that he would get well by Easter. When our Easter-weekend school break came, our family was going to take a little trip to Fontana Village, a little resort beside Fontana Lake. Since we normally never went anywhere, this seventy-mile trip really was a big deal.

Joe had a complaint: "Unless I get well, I am not going on that trip. Everybody in this world who knows me is calling me Chicken Boy. I am not going over to that place where a whole bunch of people who do not even know me are going to start calling me the same thing. If I do not get well by then, I am not going!"

Mama kept taking him back to the doctor's office to be checked because she wanted us to get to go on the trip.

It was the Thursday afternoon before Easter. That was the day that the doctor declared that Joe was healed and removed the strapping from his shoulders. He came home as happy as a child could be. "I'm not Chicken Boy anymore, I'm not Chicken Boy anymore," he kept repeating as he waved his now-free arms around and around.

As soon as Mama got him home from the doctor's office, she called Daddy at work. "We can go!" she gushed. "He's well."

"That's great. I expected that." Daddy was always the optimist. "Here's a good idea. What if I take the day off tomorrow and we start on the trip a day early? I'll call and get it all fixed up, and you go ahead and pack for all of us."

Mama was happy.

Joe and I wanted to help her pack. There were a lot of our things that we needed to be sure ended up in the car on the way. After all, the trip was going to take nearly two hours, and we needed lots of things to make such an infinite duration pass.

Mama was frustrated. "You boys are in my way. Why don't you go outside and play so I can get this packing done for our trip? Now, go on!"

Joe and I headed outside. He was still swinging his arms around and singing, "I'm not Chicken Boy anymore."

We walked around toward the back of the house, and there, right across the fence from us, we saw Larry and Ronnie playing in their backyard. "Hey, Ronnie. Hey, Larry. I'm not Chicken Boy anymore."

That was all that it took. It was Larry who suggested it: "Want to play football?" We were on the way.

Back now in our front yard, we chose up teams. As always, it ended up with Larry and me against Joe and Ronnie. We lined up for the kickoff—away from the window, of course. I held the ball. Larry ran and kicked. The ball tumbled end over end through the air.

No one in the world would ever have believed that my brother, Joe, might have caught the ball again. No one ever had to believe such a thing because he didn't. Ronnie caught the ball.

Ronnie seemed to know exactly what to do. He instantly handed the ball off to Joe, and with a burst of speed he turned and ran the other way. Larry and I had no choice; we jumped on Joe and smashed him into the ground.

He was crying before we could get off of him. Joe rolled over, but he could not get up from the ground. All his left arm could do was to drag along behind the rest of his body. We had broken his other collarbone. Larry and Ronnie ran home before Mama got out there. I tried to help Joe carry his loose arm over to the car to wait for her to take him back to the hospital.

In a couple of hours, Chicken Boy was back home again.

We did not have the trip to Fontana Village. But we did have a little show at home that night. It was at the dinner table. It was a show between Mama and Daddy, but it also included the rest of us.

Mama's emotions had now all turned from worry to anger. She was mad about both broken collarbones (even though the first one had already healed), and for some reason she was mad at me! It didn't even seem to matter that Larry had been in on it, too. No, it was declared to be totally my fault.

"What were you thinking about? I know the answer: 'Nothing.' That is the answer. You were not thinking at all. What are you trying to do? Break all of your brother's bones? Do you want me to make you a bone chart so you can break one, check it off, break the next one, check it off? They think that you are smart at school. That just shows what they know at school!"

Daddy couldn't hold it any longer. He burst out laughing, almost doubled over on the kitchen table. He couldn't help himself. He simply shook with deep laughs.

Instantly, Mama's anger shifted its focus. Now, Daddy was the target. "This is not funny, mister! What are you laughing about? You are just like your son: you think you are smart and are not! Well, look at your son. Look at him and tell him right now how smart you think he is!" She was red in the face.

Daddy looked peacefully at me. He thought for a moment, then he started: "Son, you are smart. I will even tell you how smart you are. You are so very smart that you know better than to break your *own* bones the way your mama did it!"

That was all that was said. Mama almost passed out, but she could say nothing at all. There she sat, more than thirty years later, with the break bumps still on her arms. She was totally silent . . . for several days!

That Sunday afternoon, everyone ended up out in the yard. Larry and Ronnie even came over when they saw that Joe was alive and seemed to be looking well.

Daddy called the four of us together. "Well, boys," he started slowly. "I wanted to talk with you. It seems that we have some new rules for football. Actually, only one new rule. Pay attention: *no more football!*" And that was it.

And . . . the big front window never did get broken.

Chapter 15

TWO RED COATS

When our father was born in 1901, he was number eight of thirteen siblings. By the time he was nineteen years old, he was the oldest one still close to home. His older brothers and sister were grown or married or out on their own and into their own lives. So when their father suddenly died, he was the available unmarried child ready to take over the family.

For more than the next twenty years, he took care of his mother, took care of his aunt Laura, and finished raising his own five little brothers and sisters. He sent four of the five of them to college. He told me once that he "got to be forty years old, and just forgot to get married." I didn't think he forgot. I thought he simply didn't have time to think about it.

When he was into his early forties, he met my mother, a twenty-five-year-old schoolteacher. They fell in love and ran away and got married. (I later learned from him that the reason they ran away was that he was almost the same age as his new mother-in-law. He thought he and Mama had better hide out for a few days before they came back so it was too late to undo what had happened.)

So my brother, Joe, and I grew up in a slightly unusual household. Our mother, the oldest of nine children, was now going to be sure that her own children knew how to do the right thing, no matter what. In contrast, our father was now about ready to become a grandfather, and he thought that most of the things we did to annoy our mother were simply funny. His suggestions and his own childhood stories added to our amusement.

In that world, our father seemed to have two main hobbies. One of his hobbies could be called "spoiling our mother." The equally important second hobby would have to be called "annoying our mother." He was such a genius at the practice of these two hobbies that he could often manage to effect both ends in a single event.

One of the times I most enjoyed watching him practice these hobbies came on Christmas morning when Mama opened the present he had carefully selected just for her. Watching this opening, and her reaction to it, was almost as much fun as opening my own presents.

I was about seven or eight years old when I first began to observe the pattern of gift giving. That year, I watched as Mama opened a beautifully wrapped long box, and there, all laid out before her eyes, was a perfectly matched set of seven yellow-handled screwdrivers. There was even a little rack that could be mounted on the wall so that, whenever she had need of a screwdriver, all she had to do was reach out and choose the right one for the job. She was so emotionally overcome by this gift that she could not say anything. I could read on her face the depth to which she was impressed by Daddy's shopping skills.

One year, she got a bright red wheelbarrow with an inflated

rubber tire. Another year, she got a yellow McCulloch chain saw. As she opened it, Daddy sang the theme song: "You're in luck when you got a McCulloch chain saw!" She was almost as impressed with the music as she was with the gift itself.

I am certain that she was the first woman on our entire side of town to have her very own weed eater.

One particular year, however, stands out above all the rest. It was the year when I was eleven years old. That year, Christmas morning came, and as soon as breakfast was finished, wrapped gifts were opened.

Mama picked up a long and heavy box. She pulled off the ribbon and tore off the paper. The box said, "Turner's Department Store." Mama was excited. This had the possibility of being a different kind of year. When the lid came off the box, she screamed, "You got it! You got it!" As she was screeching, she was lifting from the box a bright red, full-length wool overcoat. It was indeed beautiful.

Mama squeezed into the new coat and marched all around the living room. "It is beautiful, it is so beautiful," she chanted over and over again. "Oh, Joe, how in the world did you know that I wanted this?"

I was only eleven years old, and I clearly knew the answer to that question. Daddy and Joe and I had watched her try on the red coat at Turner's Store at least fifty times since September. If he couldn't figure out by now that she wanted it, then he really was dumb.

Now, it was his turn to ask a question: "Did I get the right size?"

Mama wiggled around in the tight coat and seemed to try to pull her shoulders together in the front. Even an eleven-year-old boy could tell that she needed at least one full size larger. But she was so flattered that he had chosen the little one that she wasn't about to say anything about it. "It's beautiful!" Mama admired herself without actually answering his direct question.

In a little while, it was time to go to my aunt Eddie's house. The next younger of Mama's six little sisters, Aunt Eddie (and Uncle David) lived nearby. This year, it was their turn to host both the local and out-of-town relatives for the Christmas Day family gathering. We loaded food and family presents and headed out in the Plymouth.

Arriving at Aunt Eddie and Uncle David's house, Daddy pulled into the front yard with the other family cars that were already there. He and Joe gathered the presents from the backseat and started toward the house, while Mama and I went back to the trunk to get the food we had brought.

Our offering was totally predictable. (One of us children once asked, "Mama, can you make deviled eggs if you're not even going anywhere?") Deviled eggs rode in the appropriately shaped Tupperware carrier, encircling green lime Jell-O with grated cheese and pineapple in the center. There was also Mama's fried chicken with my special wishbone piece already hidden under the cloth napkin lining the basket in which it was being carried.

While we were getting the food out of the car trunk, I noticed something. "Mama," I needed to warn her, "you didn't take the tags off your new coat. They're hanging right there. Do you want me to pull them off for you?" I was looking at two rather large slick-paper tags hanging by short strings, one on each side of the new coat.

"Shhh!" Mama's finger was up to her mouth as she quickly stuffed the still-attached tags into the side pockets of the coat. "Don't tell your daddy. It's too little. I just squeezed into it today for his benefit. On Monday, I am going to take it up to Turner's

Store and swap it for the right size. That's why it needs to have the tags left on it."

"Oh," I agreed.

We carried our food containers and went up to the front door. Since Daddy and Joe had gone into the house already, Aunt Eddie knew that we had arrived. Just as we got to the front door, she met us there. She saw Mama's coat and squealed, "You got it! Oh, look, you got it!" She and Mama had been both trying on the coats at Turner's Store. They both wanted the same thing.

"Did you get one, too?" Mama asked the question.

Aunt Eddie chuckled. "We have been working so hard getting ready for everybody to come today that we have not opened a single present. But you know very well that David Boyd did not spend enough money on a present to buy me a coat like that."

"Try mine on, Eddie," Mama offered. "It's too little for me. I'm going to swap it on Monday. I bet it will fit you just right."

Mama and Eddie looked a whole lot alike except that Mama was, at this time, at least a good full size larger than Eddie. Aunt Eddie put on the red coat, and it fit her perfectly. She marched around and around admiring herself in the reflecting glass of the front windows, then removed the coat and handed it back to Mama. "It really is beautiful, and warm, too!"

Aunt Eddie took our food back toward the kitchen while we put all of our coats in that place that is built for them: we put them in a pile on the bed in the front bedroom. Then we followed her to the kitchen to start into a semester of eating.

I looked around the kitchen and took my own roll call of the people gathered there. There were my grandparents, Mama's mama and daddy. There was Mama and her six little sisters. There was Daddy and the other six brothers-in-law who had married that covey of women. There was my uncle Spencer and his wife,

Betty. There was my uncle Steve, not yet nearly old enough to get married. There was a whole passel of what was coming to be more than a dozen cousins. Food was everywhere and in great abundance.

Our father was the oldest of the brothers-in-law, and the most influential. His hobby of annoying our mama had spread to the others, and no family gathering ever occurred without some sort of planned embarrassment being publicly played out for all to see. The memories of such events were abundant, especially at times of gift giving.

I remember the year when Aunt Nancy got her new teeth. Aunt Nancy's reputation, earned or not, was that she never stopped talking. With her new teeth, she could talk better than ever. That year of the new teeth, she opened a Christmas present, and out came a set of wind-up teeth that clattered and chattered and bounced all over the table. "Look, Nancy," one of the brothers-in-law stated, "those are the teeth you were supposed to get. They're the only ones that can keep up with your mouth!"

There was another year when Aunt Betty opened a package, and out came some sort of garment. She held it up, and everyone saw that it was a large, baggy pair of drawers made out of dishcloths. Pinned to the seat of the drawers was a poem that read,

> If you do not like wearing these britches,
> Then step right out and wash the dishes!

There was always an embarrassing trick in the air. What would it be this time?

Everyone had eaten a serving or two when Uncle David (Aunt Eddie's husband) and another one of the uncles sidled out of the kitchen. There was so much going on that no one noticed. They just quietly eased out. The two of them headed to the front bedroom, where they found Mama's new red coat. They then hunted up a box of the right size, folded the coat carefully into the box, and wrapped it up as a Christmas present from Uncle David to Aunt Eddie. Then the new "present" went under the Christmas tree in the living room.

Soon, it was time to open all of the presents. Everyone moved out of the kitchen and gathered in the living room. To make it all last longer, one present at a time was opened in front of everyone, with the name of the giver being read out loud for proper credit. This could last for a long time.

In no time, ribbons and wrapping paper were flying everywhere. There were cousin presents and grandparent presents and brother-sister presents of all kinds. It was a glorious day.

One of the sisters picked up the long, heavy box and read the name aloud: "Eddie, this one's for you. I can't imagine what it is. It is so heavy!"

The package was handed over. Everyone was watching as Aunt Eddie pulled off the ribbon and tore into the paper. When the lid came off the box, she and Mama screamed at the same time.

"You got one, too!"

"I got one, too!"

In no time, the red coat—the one that fit her perfectly—was out of the box, and Aunt Eddie had slipped into it. Then she went running over to Uncle David, almost crying. Her arms were around his neck. "It is so beautiful! Thank you, thank you, thank you!" She gave him a kiss.

Uncle David had a funny look on his face. This was not at all what was expected. He looked like a person who had just realized that he had stepped into something he was not sure he wanted stuck to his foot.

Aunt Eddie would not take the coat off. She wore it all over the house, showing it over and over again to everyone and soliciting their admiration. I thought that she might even end up sleeping in it that night.

Pretty soon, everything was over and it was time to go home. We headed into the front bedroom to get our coats. One of them was not there!

Mama stood there looking at the empty bed and thinking about things. She was the oldest of all the sisters, and she knew everything there was to know and understand about them and the fellows to whom they were married. It took her only a few seconds to figure out both what had happened and what she was going to do about it. She grinned to herself, then put on a serious face as she marched out into the living room.

"David Boyd!" She spoke to him in a voice that got everyone's attention. "Something terrible has happened at your house while we were all enjoying our Christmas dinner. You have left every door and window in this house unlocked and half open, and while we were having a good time some evil, wandering scoundrel has come into your house and stolen my new coat. It is gone from the bedroom!"

Uncle Ralph laughed out loud. Uncle David tried to laugh but couldn't quite manage it. Finally, he blustered, "It's not stolen. Eddie's wearing it! You know how we like to do tricks. It's not stolen. Eddie's got it on!"

With an extremely stern look on her face, Mama looked at Aunt Eddie as she spoke to Uncle David. "You stop teasing Eddie like that, David. Look how much she loves that coat that you got her. And besides that, look how it fits her. I am bigger than Eddie. I could not even squeeze into that coat. And another thing . . . Eddie's new coat still has the tags hanging on the sides of it. You don't think I would have come out here with the new tags hanging on my coat like Minnie Pearl's hat, do you? Now, you stop teasing Eddie!"

With that, Mama gathered us up, and we walked out the door and went home. Uncle David was left standing there strangely and oddly speechless. Uncle Ralph could not stop laughing.

Nothing was said in the car all the way home, but Mama seemed to be humming a little happy tune to herself all the while.

When we got home, the telephone started ringing just as we got inside the house. Mama simply said, seemingly to herself, "I think it worked." Then she answered the telephone.

It was Aunt Eddie. She was talking so loudly that we could hear it all over the room. "Oh, Lucille," she gushed, "I cannot believe that David got me this beautiful coat. He has never spent that much money on me in my life. It is just perfect! But he is feeling so terrible that someone came in our house and stole your new coat. He is so upset that he couldn't even talk with you. He wanted me to call you to see whether you might know of anyplace where he could get you another one."

The end of the story came on the following Monday. I still remember going with quite a number of other relatives to watch while, at Turner's Department Store, Uncle David laid down forty-one dollars to buy Mama the red coat that fit her exactly right. And that was the last time any of those brothers-in-law tried to play holiday tricks on the sisters whom they had married.

The next Christmas, Daddy got Mama a silver bullet-shaped Electrolux vacuum cleaner. When she opened the gigantic box and saw what was inside, she burst out, "Oh, Joe. How did you ever know that I needed one of these?"

"It was easy," Daddy replied with a smile. "Eddie already has one!"

Chapter 16

THE LAST WHOOPING

Whenever punishment happened at home, it was almost always Mama who meted it out. Her well-known switch bush sometimes had a hard time living through the summer, as it was pruned regularly to secure the harvest of switches she needed to handle two boys through the weeks when we were out of school.

If we ever had to be punished by our father, it was a dire situation. Usually, he thought everything that we did was funny, and even helped us at times avoid Mama's switches. But on occasion, he was called into action. The nature of these rare times of paternal punishment led us to eventually have two totally different labels for what we were up against. If the punishment came from Mama, it was called "a switching." If we had to get it from Daddy, it was a certified "whooping."

Even our neighbors Larry and Ronnie knew about the "whooping" label—probably because when punishment came from their father, it deserved the same title.

Before we moved to live next door to the Leatherwoods when

I was twelve and Joe was nine, we had lived at our old house on Plott Creek Road. Though we looked up at Eagles' Nest Mountain, all the creek-bottom land around that house was totally flat. It never occurred to us at that house to beg for sleds for Christmas. When it did snow, there were no hills at all for us to even dream about sliding down. On Plott Creek, our snow activity was focused on building snowmen or throwing snowballs.

We moved to the new house in the summertime, and though we immediately began playing with Larry and Ronnie, we still did not notice that this new location had a totally different topography for winter play. Our house and the Leatherwoods' house shared a long hilltop. In almost every direction, the hill dropped down from the two houses—perfect for winter sledding.

By the time cold weather came, we were already talking with Larry and Ronnie about what would happen when it snowed. They showed us that the very best hill for sledding was the old pasture hill behind their house. There was no longer a cow in that whole pasture, and the hill came down, down, down, then turned back uphill at the bottom to naturally stop you before you hit the fence. It was made for us.

Starting in about September, Joe and I both began begging for sleds for Christmas. We also hoped that all of the snow that might be planning to fall this winter would wait until after we got our sleds, so we could take full advantage of them.

The snow held off, Christmas came, and so did the sleds. Santa did not fail us! Joe and I got two sleds. Both were Flexible Flyers. Mine was long, and his was short. I think that Santa thought that sleds came in sizes like boys did—a tall one for me and a shorter one for my little brother. Actually, the longer sled worked well for two riders, but it was not as fast if only one person was on it as was the short, small sled that Joe got. We swapped them around so much that neither one really had anyone's name attached to it.

Not only did the sleds come on Christmas Day, so did the snow. It started about dusk that afternoon. It was a disappointing-looking start. It was not huge, flat, feathery flakes. No, it started as tiny, grainy-looking little balls of snow. It really didn't look like it was going to amount to anything.

When we complained about the snow, Mama told us that, no, it was actually the best kind. "If it starts off big," her opinion was offered, "it never ends up amounting to anything. But you watch out now. With this kind of little start, there will be as much snow as you want by morning."

She was right! The next morning, we looked out the window at daylight and discovered that the entire world was deeply white. It had started out looking like a dry snow, but as it accumulated, the flakes must have gotten bigger. Now, it was a perfect ten inches of good, slick, wet, perfect-for-sledding snow.

It was hard to eat breakfast before going outside. We looked out our kitchen window and could see that there were already tracks from the Leatherwoods' house out toward the old cow pasture. Larry and Ronnie were waiting for us.

It was torture to have to get dressed the way Mama made us do it. We had on so many clothes we could hardly bend our joints. Finally, we were ready for our first trials of the new sleds.

Larry and Ronnie were ready when we got over there. "You've got to break them in before they really go," Larry advised. "I've brought some wax for the runners." He held up a block of paraffin that he had snatched from his mother's canning supplies from the summer. "Keep rubbing this on the runners every time you get back to the top, and as the new paint wears off of the runners, you will get faster and faster." We were in business.

The only obstacle on the whole hill was one old apple tree. It was right in the middle of the field and about halfway down the big hill. What we did was slide down on one side of the tree and walk back up the other side for a while, then reverse the whole order of things. It was not really a problem at all.

For a while, we each rode our own sleds. Larry and Ronnie's older sleds were faster, as the runners were polished free of all paint and had been waxed over and over again. Neither of them had a long sled like the one I had gotten.

Pretty soon, we were trying it out with two people riding. It seemed like the thing to do was for two people to sit up on the sled, instead of lying flat on your belly the way one rider would do it. That way, the person in front could steer by putting his feet on the sled handles. When we tried it this way, however, our center of gravity was so high that we always fell off before we managed to get to the bottom of the hill.

Soon, we figured out that the way to do it was to put whoever was bigger on his belly on the bottom and whoever was smaller flat on top of him. The bottom person steered, and the one on top just held on for dear life. We soon got pretty good at this.

The four of us had been out on the hill for a couple of hours when one of the little brothers had to go to the bathroom. As soon as one of them got the idea, the other one realized that he, too, had to go. Larry and I told them to go in the snow—that you could actually write your name in the snow and it would show up yellow. They were shy and thought that was nasty. So they both decided to go in the Leatherwoods' house for a bathroom break.

Larry and I waited. We were looking down the hill and talking, and suddenly one of us had an inspired idea. We got the long Flexible Flyer. It had a rope loop on the front that ended in knots through both steering handles. The rope was what you used to pull the sled back up the hill. We worked out the plan. The little boys were in no hurry to come back, so we had plenty of time.

"Get on the sled," Larry said to me. "I've got hold of the rope."

I got on the sled on my belly. While Larry used the rope to hold the sled back like a leash held a dog, I steered the sled as we let it make tracks in the fresh snow straight toward the one apple tree.

As soon as the nose of the sled was right at the tree, I got off the sled, trying to step in the snow as far from it as I could, so my tracks would be mixed in with old tracks. Larry and I then carefully picked up the sled. We let it down at an angle so that a runner was sitting in one track that had come down the hill, and extended this track past the apple tree on one side of the tree. Then we moved to the other side and extended the other track past the tree on its own side. After that, we put the sled back down in the snow so it fit right in the two tracks that now extended past and were below the tree. It looked exactly like the sled had gone right through that tree.

The little boys were coming back. We could hear them talking. Larry and I both got on the sled. Just as they came into sight, we pushed off and screamed, "We did it, we did it! We rode through the tree!" We sped on down through the fresh snow to the bottom of the hill.

Joe and Ronnie could not believe it, but they had practically seen us do it. And there in front of everyone was the clear evidence: two sled runner tracks started at the top of the hill, they came down toward the apple tree, one went on each side of the tree, and they had actually seen us as it looked like we finished the ride to the bottom of the hill.

It was so clear that Larry and I did not even have to suggest it. They wanted to try. "How do you do it?" one of them asked.

We were eager to give advice: "You have to hit it right in the middle. You have to be going as fast as you can. You need to close your eyes at the last moment. You have to *believe!*"

The two of us watched, trying not to smile, as the little brothers loaded up at the top of the hill. They started down the slope, one on top of the other, going faster and faster. All of a sudden, Larry and I had twin unanticipated attacks of conscience. At the same time, we started running down the hill toward them, hollering, "*Nooo! Nooo!* Stop!" It was all too late. All we were doing was announcing to our little brothers that they had been tricked and that we were guilty.

Luckily, their aim was not as good as we told them it needed to be. They did not quite center the tree. It was bad enough, though. The big sled came to a cracking dead stop. They did not stop, but each one hit a good part of the tree. They ended up with knots on each head.

Blame and bad language were exchanged, punctuated by tears, for a good little while. (Maybe it would have been better had they been knocked out.) And on this first day of its life, my sled had a bent crossbar on the front of it. But it had all been worth it.

Larry and I knew that we were going to be in bad trouble. It never happened. The little brothers were so ashamed that they had been taken in by us that they did not tell on us. They even managed to hide the visible damage so that no convicting questions were ever asked by our parents.

We were sure that we had gotten away with it . . . we thought.

It was probably March, and Larry and I had forgotten all about the sled/tree incident. On a Sunday night, as usual, all four of us boys were at one house watching television before bedtime. It was a Disney show and the feature was about Davy Crockett. Then, at one point in the program, Davy Crockett and his buddies were digging a pit and covering it with sticks and leaves in order to trap a bear for them to eat. It was great.

The next day, Larry and I were talking about the bear pit. That's when the idea came to us. We could dig a pit like that, but not for bears. We could dig a pit and catch our little brothers. (Why we wanted to do this, we were not sure. It never came up. It just seemed like a good idea.)

The sledding hill was behind the Leatherwoods' house. It was all open pastureland, and you could not hide anything there. But on the opposite side of our house, the hill was either wooded or at least grown over with brushy vegetation. We often played hideout sorts of games there when the weather was good. It was the perfect place.

That Saturday, the little brothers were watching cartoons on television, so Larry and I started our plan. We went down onto the grown-up hillside and chose a place out of sight below the edge of Daddy's garden. We marked off a square about eight or nine feet on a side and started to dig.

The soil was a loose sandy clay mix. It was easy to shovel. We had picked a place away from big trees so we would not have to deal with any roots. It was good.

The only problem we had was what to do with all the dirt we dug out of the hole. The top layer that had grassy stuff growing on it we carefully kept to the side. We figured we would need it to help disguise the trap later.

It was springtime, and both of our fathers had recently had their side-by-side gardens plowed. They were just above us on the top of the hill. The dirt up there looked just like the dirt down here. So Larry and I dug the sandy clay into a big bucket, and, taking turns doing the carrying, we carried each bucket of dirt up to one of the garden plots and scattered it all around so it would never be noticed. It was hard work but a good plan.

Over a period of a few weeks, we dug the pit deeper and deeper. In a short time, we had to take a small stepladder from our garage down to the pit so we could get both the dirt and ourselves out of it as it deepened. Before long, we had the pit deep enough that no one could climb out of it without our help. Now, we were ready.

Larry and I carefully put pine limbs over the pit. Then we added fallen pine needles and leftover leaves from the winter. We used the old sod we had saved to cover the ends of the pine boughs so no one would see them. We had done a job that would have done Davy Crockett proud.

That Saturday, we asked our little brothers, "Want to go outside and play? It's getting to be springtime now. We can play down in the woods."

"What do you want to play?" they asked.

"Let's play 'Wild Animals in the Woods.' " I made up the name.

"What does that mean?" one of them asked.

"It means that we each choose a wild animal to be, and then we chase each other all over the place to see which animal can catch which animal. It will be fun."

They agreed. We chose up to be lion, tiger, bear, and jaguar.

Larry and I chased Joe and Ronnie all over the hillside, but they simply would not run over the top of the pit. We got them to chase us, but they only followed right in our tracks. We could not trap them, and we surely did not want to catch ourselves. We abandoned that plan in the middle of an argument about which of these animals could beat the other ones.

We needed a new plan.

The coming weekend was Easter—time for the Easter egg

hunt. It had possibilities. All four of us agreed to work on our eggs together and then combine them for the hunt, so there would be a lot more. We worked most of Good Friday decorating eggs. The big hunt was to be on Sunday afternoon after church and Easter Sunday dinner.

It was a beautiful April Easter afternoon. Both families, parents and kids, gathered on the back porch of our house to get ready for the egg hunt. The parents had us flip a coin to see who would hide the eggs first. Larry and I won the right to hide the eggs, and we were off.

There were two dozen eggs to hide. We hid some of them so thoroughly that the next summer I hit two rotten eggs when I was trimming at the edge of the yard with the lawn mower. We hid some eggs in the yard and others down on the hillside. Twenty-three of the eggs were deeply out of sight and took real work to find. The twenty-fourth egg was totally visible. It was out in the open, right in the center of the covering of the little-boy trap. They had to fall now.

Joe and Ronnie searched until their time was up. They found over twenty of the eggs we had hidden. One of those they never seemed to see was the purple-and-yellow egg that was perched over the pit. We just couldn't seem to get them to fall in it in any way in the world.

After both sides hid the eggs and the others had looked for them twice, we were tired of the egg hunt. Besides, our eggs were now down to nineteen with the recurring inability to find them all and the simultaneous forgetfulness about where they were hidden. We had a great afternoon.

Way in the afternoon, Daddy and Mr. Leatherwood were poking around to see if they could find any of the eggs we had totally lost. All of a sudden, Mr. Leatherwood jumped back and warned Daddy, "Watch out, Joe. There's a yellow jackets' nest here at the base of this little dogwood tree. It's in the ground and looks like it's about the size of a gallon jar. We better burn it out."

Mr. Leatherwood walked over to their house to get the kerosene while Daddy watched the yellow jackets' nest as if to be sure it didn't move.

In no time, our neighbor was back with a quart jar of kerosene and a few wooden strike-anywhere matches. It was almost sunset, and the yellow jackets were coming home and settling down for the night. Our fathers watched the nest for a while to be sure the residents were home and settled. Joe and Ronnie got tired of waiting for this, so they headed in the house to watch television.

Finally, all was calm.

"Watch this, boys," Larry's daddy warned. "We've got to be quick!"

He then squatted on the ground beside the buried nest, reached out with the jar of kerosene, and poured quite a generous dose down and into the nest. That alone might have killed them, but it was, on this day, not enough.

Then Mr. Leatherwood pulled one of the wooden matches out of his shirt pocket, struck it on the sole of his shoe, and dropped it on the kerosene-soaked yellow jackets' nest. What followed was beautiful. The nest, itself being almost the same as paper, had absorbed all the kerosene. Now, it burned like a torch. We watched as a few early yellow jackets tried to fly away, only to succumb to the combination of fire, heat, and smoke being generated. Smoke was everywhere.

Suddenly, here came the little brothers, running like the wind. "What's going on?" they asked. "We saw all that smoke from inside the house and headed out here to see what had happened."

Daddy and Mr. Leatherwood were standing there. They were

watching the fire until it was all out. "It's nothing, boys. Lawrence and I were just burning an old yellow jackets' nest. It's almost out now."

It was later that evening when Larry and I got the idea: "That smoke really did bring those little guys running. Did you see them coming out of the house? What we need is to generate some smoke to bait our trap."

I got the idea. Every time Daddy started a fire in our fireplace, before he lit the wood, he would roll up some old newspaper and light it. He would let the newspaper burn and let its smoke go up the chimney a little bit before he lit the wood. He called this "warming up the chimney to make it draw." The newspaper always produced a lot of white smoke.

Larry and I hunted up some old newspaper and waited for the next morning. It was Easter Monday, and school was out—a perfect day for our final victory.

We waited until late morning, until it was warm and pleasant to be outdoors. Larry and I got Joe and Ronnie to play a couple of games with us. Then, when they went off on their own, we got ready to start the smoke signals. We got another piece of newspaper to use to light the paper in the pit and took wooden matches with us.

Once down on the hillside, we were again impressed with the good job we had done concealing the pit. If we ourselves did not know exactly where it was, even we would not have seen it.

Once at the edge of the camouflage, we knelt down, raked back the grass and leaves, and separated two of the pine boughs. Looking deep down into the darkness, Larry and I wadded a mass of old newspaper and dropped it into the hole.

Satisfied that we had enough in the hole, I held the last piece of paper while Larry struck the wooden match on a rock.

The paper blazed up, then settled down to burn. I dropped it down the hole. We could see by its light that it landed right on the clump of wadded paper we had already dropped to the bottom.

Quickly, Larry and I repaired the opening and hid behind two trees. It would happen very soon.

For a few minutes, there was no smoke. We almost wondered whether the burning paper had gone out or the paper in the bottom was so old it was too damp to ignite. Then it started to happen. It seemed as if the smoke had simply built up until it filled the entire pit before beginning to seep through the leaves at the top. Then it began to evenly waft through all over the hidden surface of our trap. It was a big smoky area for sure. Smoke gradually rose up silently into the air. The little boys had to be coming soon. Surely, they could see this from wherever they were. Why weren't they coming?

There were two important things that Larry and I did not know. The first one was that Ronnie and Joe were no longer playing outside. They had retreated into the house to watch television. The second, and more important, thing we did not realize was that, since this was Easter Monday, our fathers were home from work. My daddy and Mr. Leatherwood were both working on top of the hill in their side-by-side gardens while Larry and I were hopefully watching a growing column of smoke rising into the sky.

Suddenly, I heard Mr. Leatherwood's voice. He was calling to my daddy. "Joe, look down there in the trees. There's smoke coming up out of the woods. We must not have gotten the yellow jackets' nest put out last night. It looks like the fire might have come back to life."

Daddy responded, "I see it. Looks like it's pretty big. Come on, Lawrence! Let's get down there and stomp it out!"

Larry and I watched from our behind-tree hideouts as my father (the vice president of First National Bank) and Larry's father (the county school superintendent) came charging downhill to stomp out the escaped fire. We stood there and silently watched.

If we had stayed hidden, maybe they would not have known who dug the big hole. But there would have lingered a lasting question: who did it? Maybe at best we might have escaped a little longer.

It was not to be so. When our fathers were no more than twenty-five feet from the pit, Larry and I were both struck by another responsibility virus. We jumped out from behind the trees and at the same time yelled, "*Nooo! Stop!*" It was too late. All we did was again announce ourselves as the culprits.

Larry and I stood there and watched as our fathers disappeared into the depths of the earth. It was an astounding and memorable image.

All kinds of things happened then: limbs flew up in the air out of the big hole, burning pieces of newspaper and grass flew out, dirt clods flew out, many very bad words flew out. There was fury in the ground!

We realized they were talking to us. "Get over here right now!" Was it Larry's daddy or mine whose voice we heard? "You heard us. Get over here and get us out of here!" It didn't matter which one it was, they were both yelling at both of us. "We are going to whoop you both. You are going to get a whooping you are going to remember. Get over here!"

Slowly, we walked over to the ruined pit and looked down into the hole. It looked like daddies-in-a-blender! They were furious. "Get us out of here!" they were both hollering now.

Suddenly, Larry and I realized the same thing at the same time. They were stuck! They could not get out of the hole without our help! We were not as close to death as we had thought. We needed to think about this whole thing.

Suddenly, Larry got the idea that our fathers' inability to get out of the hole gave him some sort of bargaining power. He looked down at both of them. "We'll get you out if you don't give us a whooping! Yes, we will!"

With that offer, both fathers got tickled. It was such a ridiculous scene that they started laughing. Then we started laughing. Then all four of us fell into laughing so hard that we were crying and could not stop. Suddenly, we were all four the same age—not fathers and sons but four boys, all of whom were in love with trouble. It was a great feeling. They then told us that they would not give us a whooping. They would think of something else for us. (We didn't even hear that last part.)

Larry and I walked up to the garage of our house and got the wooden stepladder. We carried it down to the pit and lowered it down the side. My daddy first and then Mr. Leatherwood climbed out of the hole and dusted themselves off. We were still laughing.

"Thank you, boys." It was Mr. Leatherwood talking. "We couldn't have gotten out of there without you. There is not going to be a whooping. We are good for our promise."

We were relieved, but not for long.

"While you boys were getting the ladder, we figured out what to do in place of the whooping."

We were both shocked to realize that they had really meant this promise. Larry and I listened.

We finally asked, "What is it?" We couldn't believe this was not over.

"Well"—Daddy was the speaker—"first we need to ask you, are you sure, totally sure, that you don't want a whooping?"

Larry and I did not even consult before we answered in unison, "We don't want a whooping!"

"Well," Daddy went on, "if you are sure, you can hear our plan. Here it is: this winter, the first time it snows, we want both of you boys to take a sled out on the hill over there and show the little boys how you ride the sled through the apple tree. And if you have trouble doing it the first time, we want you to do it over and over again until you get it right."

In unison, Larry and I both wailed, "Please, give us a whooping!"

Daddy and Mr. Leatherwood walked over to a maple tree, and each of them broke off a limb. They then pretended to give us a whooping, with all four of us laughing all the way through the little charade. It was wonderful punishment!

And that was the last time either of us remembered getting a whooping from either of our fathers.

Chapter 17

THE DUCKTAIL

From the time I was born until I was old enough to go to Mrs. Rosemary's kindergarten, Mama tried to cut my hair. She didn't want to waste the money to send a child to the barber and spend good money on what didn't matter anyway. While she was so totally in love with my brother Joe's hair, she thought what I got on my head (which she often compared to her own hair as "little fine mouse hair") needed to be as mowed down as possible.

Her efforts were not very successful, as I had two strongly opinionated cowlicks, one at the crown and one on the right front corner, that believed themselves to be in charge of my hair. No matter what Mama tried, it did not work. The more she cut, the worse it looked. The cowlicks made the hair stick up more and more the shorter it was.

When I was about to go out in public and be in kindergarten each day, Mama gave up. One day, she told Daddy, "Take him on down to the barbershop and get his hair cut. Maybe they can do something with it."

Daddy took me to his own barber, Herschel Caldwell. All the Caldwells came from Cataloochee, and our family had known all of them forever. Both Herschel and his brother, J. R., were barbers.

Herschel saw immediately what the problem was: Mama was trying to keep my hair so short that it would not lie down anywhere near where the cowlicks were in control. He trimmed me a little bit around the ears, then sent me back home with Daddy to tell Mama to let my hair grow out until it got enough length and weight to lie down. Then, he said, it could be parted and combed and would look very nice.

Hair was a battle with Mama all through elementary school. She still fussed when it got the least bit long, and she would always take me to the barbershop and try to supervise Herschel while he was cutting it. "Can't you take a little bit more off on top?" She was circling his chair while he cut.

"If I take more off on the top, Lucille, it will stick up at the crown like Alfalfa on *The Little Rascals*."

"Can't you make it a little shorter in the front?" She would not give up.

"If I make it shorter in the front, that part will stick up like Dagwood Bumstead." Herschel wanted to be proud of his work. The biggest embarrassment to me was simply having my mama not only take me to the barbershop but also try to supervise the barber, who knew very well what he was doing.

In about the third grade, I discovered Wildroot Cream Oil. My first little bottle was given to me by Mama's brother, my uncle Spencer. I think he felt sorry for me. I loved it.

By now, Herschel had convinced Mama that my head would actually look better if he could leave enough hair for me to comb.

The Wildroot Cream Oil did make it possible for me to get it to stick together enough for parting to happen, and it would often even lie down in the back.

I remember the day I got that first bottle. I put it in my pocket and took the Wildroot Cream Oil to school with me. All day long in Miss Ruth Metcalf's class, I secretly worked with the Wildroot Cream Oil.

When we first got to school and the bell had not yet sounded, I went to the boys' bathroom and rubbed a bit into my hair. Combed, I went to class happy and knowing that I looked good.

What was good, however, could always be better. When we got to take our restroom break on the way out to recess, I applied more Wildroot Cream Oil. It made my hair darker, and this time combing it made it look like I had permanent little harrowed rows in a cornfield. I looked even better than before.

Throughout the day, every time there was a chance, I added more of the creamy stuff.

By the afternoon, I could reach up and put my hand on my cheek and feel the slipperiness of Wildroot Cream Oil that could no longer get a grip on the top of my head. I was simply greased.

The biggest problem was that by now Mama was teaching second grade at my school, and my route home in the afternoon was to go to her room when the bell rang and, of course, ride home with her.

I had lost my sense that the Wildroot Cream Oil had a noticeable odor. I had added it little by little and grown immune to the smell. Mama, however, smelled it before she looked closely at me. I had to surrender the bottle to her, and before we even got in the car to go home, she took me into the little bathroom beside her room and washed my head with something Haskel Davis normally used to clean the sink itself. I went home smelling like a pine tree, with all my hair sticking up like pine needles.

Hair was a continuing battle as junior-high years approached. Musicians set the mark, and some of the kids I most admired seemed to have full permission to follow. The classmate I admired most was Milas Chambers, the first person my age I ever knew who had his own guitar. He thought he was Hank Williams Number Two! His hair was something to behold.

Milas Chambers lived with his grandparents, and Mama said that is why he got to have and do anything that he wanted to do. He got the guitar in about the fifth grade, and at every school talent show he would wear a cowboy hat and play Hank Williams songs. The favorite was "Hey, Good Lookin.'" When he sang, he looked girls (and even mothers) in the audience straight in the eye and winked as he strummed on the guitar.

Mama said that he had once been in her class when she substituted in Sunday school, and she did not want me playing with him, imitating him, or even looking at him. This made him more interesting than ever.

When we all moved up from Hazelwood Elementary School to Waynesville Junior High School, Milas Chambers really hit his stride. He was converted from Hank Williams to Elvis Presley. This affected his entire demeanor.

He started wearing a lot of black clothes to school, always with the back of his shirt collar turned up. His favorite song was now "Hound Dog." He wiggled when he played the guitar and sang. But worst (or best!) of all, he let his hair grow longer, dyed it black, and had it fixed up in what Mama called "a pompadour with a ducktail." She was disgusted. I was more impressed than ever.

Milas' hair was long all over. It was parted on one side, and the side away from the part was swooped up over the top of his head like an ocean wave on which a surfboard could ride. Both sides were so long that they were swooped back over his ears like wings. The tips of these black-dyed wings met at the back of his head in what for all the world did in fact look like the tail of a duck resting on the nape of his neck.

Mama could not even stand to look at him.

His hair was the goal of my dreams.

Because my mama still took me to the barbershop even in junior high school, I fought off going as long as I could between trips. And since she was now a very busy elementary-school teacher, she would accidentally let me slip by the haircuts until my hair was almost long enough to suit me and way too long to suit her.

I still rode home with her from school each day. But now that I was at the junior high school and not at her school, I had to wait each day for her to finish her work, then drive a long mile to pick me up on the way home. My little brother, Joe, would already be in the car with her.

My favorite waiting place was on the steps of the band building. This building was between the junior- and senior-high parts of the campus and had sheltered west-side steps. As the fall moved into winter, this was the warmest outdoor waiting spot.

One afternoon, she pulled into the circular drive to pick me up and I could already see the look on her face. "You look like a sheepdog!" she announced. "I was just counting on my fingers, and it has been a full month since you had your hair cut." (My hair did and always has grown very slowly. Not my fault.) "You have got to have a haircut. I wish I had time to take you up to Herschel's today, but I just can't do it. And tomorrow, I am going to have to go to the grocery store. I hate for people to know that a child of mine looks like you do!"

That's when I got the idea. I offered, "Mama, I am thirteen years old. I know where the barbershop is located. I know Herschel Caldwell. Why don't you just give me some money, and as soon as school is out tomorrow, I can walk on into town and get my own hair cut while you go to the grocery store."

"How would you get home from there?"

I was afraid something would be wrong with this plan. "It is not much over a mile to walk home. I won't go on the highway. There is a sidewalk all the way to the hospital, then I can go up Woodland Drive and cut through Rubye and Howard Bryson's to the top of Hillside Terrace, and come on home that way. It would not be too long at all." I crossed my fingers behind my back.

Mama thought about it a few minutes. We had all once walked to town and back that way in the summer, just to see how it could be done if needed. I could easily do it.

Finally, she agreed: "I guess it's a good idea. You can try it tomorrow if it is not raining. I will send you to school with two dollars. The haircut is a dollar and sixty cents."

Of course, I already knew how much a haircut was. This was ridiculous. But it was going to work.

The next morning, I went to school with two dollars in my pocket and a plan in my head.

When the afternoon bell rang, I left Mrs. Pilarski's classroom and headed toward town. It was no distance at all. Kids walked there from school every day.

Herschel now cut hair at the Parkway Barbershop. It was a wonderful place with a half-dozen Koken chairs, mirrors covering the walls from the midpoint up on both sides, and a sign that proclaimed, "No Profanity and No Spitting." The barbershop always smelled wonderful.

When I got in the door, Herschel was cutting an old man's

hair. I recognized the old man but did not know his name. I would be next.

When he finished shaving around the old man's ears, Herschel whipped the sheet covering off him, popped the hair off of it while the man got out of the chair, and said straight to me, "Next! It's you, little Davis. How did you get here without your mama?"

I climbed up into the chair as I answered Herschel's question. "I am thirteen years old. I guess I can at least find my way to the barbershop without my mama."

Herschel chuckled. "I know you can. But I also know your mama. I've known her longer than you have. Now, what can I do for you today? Your hair is longer than she usually lets it get. Want it cut all over the way we usually do it?"

"No!" I answered quickly, before he could fire up the electric clippers. "Like I said, I am thirteen years old. I guess I can decide how I want my hair cut!"

"I guess you can." Herschel had a smile on his face now. "So, without your mama here, how do you want your hair cut?"

The answer started with a question: "Do you know Milas Chambers?"

Herschel was beaming now, but I did not realize that I was the source of his entertainment. "Of course I know Milas. I guess I know everybody in this end of Haywood County. What has Milas Chambers got to do with your haircut?"

"Everything! What I want is for my hair to look like his looks. I am not sure that any of it actually needs to be cut off . . . just *fixed*. I don't want it dyed black. I'll keep my color. I just want to have a ducktail!"

Remarkably, Herschel controlled himself. He did not laugh out loud. He calmly asked, one last time, "Is it okay with your mother for you to have your hair like that?"

This was a question that could not be answered directly. I did the best I could. "Remember what I told you? I am thirteen years old, and I guess I can get my hair fixed any way I want it fixed. It is my hair."

"You asked for it!" was Herschel's only answer.

He started. Herschel lathered the nape of my neck and shaved the bottom hair off in a straight line above the level of the shirt collar. He did the tiniest bit of trimming of my sideburns. Then he searched around the shelf behind him until he found a round container labeled, "Butch Wax." My hair was going to need all the help it could get.

Herschel globbed some of the Butch Wax into my hair. He then combed it all straight back. That is the way he figured out where the part needed to go. He heated up a metal comb as his tool of choice. I could feel the warmth of the comb as he raked the wings back above each ear. I could feel the tickle on the back of my head as he shaped the ducktail. At the end, he kept combing the pompadour straight up in the air and letting it fall back over my head until it suited him.

Before he let me look in the mirror, Herschel gave me the maintenance instructions: "You might want to get some of this Butch Wax and a metal comb. It will help your hair set up and stay in place. The problem is that your hair is just not as thick as Milas Chambers' hair. You are going to have to let it grow as much as possible. We can always square it off at the bottom. I just know your mama is going to like it!"

"How much do I owe you?" I knew that this was the question to ask, even though the rate list on the wall clearly stated all the prices.

"You do not owe me a penny!" Herschel announced to the entire barbershop. "This gave me a chance to try out something

I have wanted to try for years." (I had no idea he had such a long history of knowing my mother.) "You just take good care of yourself."

I was soon out of the chair and ready to start my walk home.

Almost every car and every person in Waynesville was someone I either actually knew or recognized as familiar. So all the way home, I was being met or passed, on foot or on wheels, by people with whom I could have talked or at least waved. On the entire half-hour walk, I was most careful to make no eye contact with any living person or moving vehicle. Something in my deep brain was telling me that no such meeting would be complimentary. It was a long walk.

Mama had a lot of shopping to do at the grocery store, and perhaps she took advantage of the trip and made other stops as well. For whatever reason, I got home a good while before she did. I did not go into any room dominated by a mirror. No, by now, there was no need to look. I already knew I had made a big mistake and was totally done for.

Suddenly, I knew what to do to redeem myself. I would cook supper for the entire family, and Mama would be so relieved she might not even notice the ducktail business. This would work.

From the freezer in the garage, I got a package of ground beef. It was frozen, but if you put it in the frying pan with the stove turned on, I knew it would gradually thaw if I kept turning it over and over and scraping the thawed part off with a spatula. I got onions and canned tomatoes. All of this would make spaghetti sauce.

A big pot of water went on to get hot for the noodles once the sauce had cooked and everyone was home and ready to eat. In the freezer, there was even a package of brown-and-serve rolls to finish off the menu.

By the time Mama's car came up the driveway, the sauce had bubbled and cooked until it was at least edible, and would be really good by the time we were actually ready to eat. The long box of spaghetti noodles was on the counter beside the ready, simmering water. The rolls were on a cookie sheet, already with butter spread on top before they went in to be browned. I knew I was safe.

Then the door opened. Mama smelled the food. It seemed to raise her curiosity more than feed her happiness. Mothers are not predictable. She stepped into the kitchen and nearly screamed, as she could see only the back of my head as I stood over the stove. She thought a stranger was cooking at our house. I turned and smiled.

She sounded like she started to pray: "Oh, dear Lord, what in the world has happened to you?"

By the time I realized it was not a prayer, things were coming apart in a hurry. Mama stepped right past me, reached out, and turned off all the knobs on the stove. She picked up the pan of spaghetti sauce and put it, hot, into the refrigerator without even putting a lid on it.

"Get in the car!" was the order. "Did Herschel Caldwell do this to you? Let's go!"

By the time our car pulled up in front of the Parkway Barbershop, it was already dark inside. We were now past closing time, and all the barbers had gone home for the night. Mama glanced at her watch to confirm the time, hit the gas, and we were off again. I could not imagine what was coming next and was not about to ask.

All of a sudden, I figured out what was happening: we were headed for Herschel's house!

We got there. Mama did not even have to tell me to come with her as she got out of the car and marched up toward the house. We did not go toward the front door. No, we headed right around to the back, where you could see lights on in what had to be the kitchen. Then came the biggest surprise: Mama did not even knock on the door. No, she simply opened it, and we were in the kitchen.

Herschel and his wife were already sitting down at their kitchen table for supper. They looked up at us. Herschel's wife looked totally perplexed. Herschel himself had a little grin on his face that told me he already knew that, whatever happened, this moment alone was worth every bit of it.

"Hello, Lucille. Would you all like to have supper with us?"

Mama pulled me in front of her into the Caldwells' direct line of vision. "Look at this mess, Herschel Caldwell. You have known me long enough to be smarter than this. You know very well that Lucille Davis would not have a child of hers going out in public looking like this. You have embarrassed the very life out of me. Now . . . *fix it!*"

Herschel's wife didn't move. She just watched with wide, wild eyes. Herschel himself smiled through the entire operation. He brought me over to the kitchen sink, ran the water until it tested properly warm, squirted a huge glob of dishwashing detergent on my head, and lathered it up. This was repeated three or four times, with lots of rinsing in between, until all of the greasy Butch Wax seemed to be gone.

He then sat me down in a kitchen chair and disappeared for a moment. Soon, he was back with a boxed set of haircutting instruments. Mama watched as Herschel carefully combed, clipped, trimmed, combed, clipped, trimmed . . . until my hair was soon too short to part or comb anymore.

"Now"—she was not quite finished with him—"give him his money back!"

Mama did not know that Herschel had not charged me for the haircut. Neither of us said a word. No, Herschel simply reached into his pocket and counted out one dollar and sixty cents and put it in my hand.

Now, it was his turn to talk. "I'm sorry about how this turned out, Lucille. I'll tell you what. I cut his hair free the next time also."

With that, Mama was satisfied, and we were gone.

She never went to the barbershop with me again. She did not need to go. No, from now on, she gave me money and I went by myself. Nor did Herschel ever again have to ask, "How do you want your hair cut today?" Both of us already knew the answer to that. From then on, I looked exactly the way my mama wanted me to look. It just wasn't worth the fight.

But every time I saw Herschel from that day to the end of his life, we each had a secret little smile for one another.

Chapter 18

BRACES

Mama had beautiful teeth, and she was proud of them! They were perfectly straight and even, a uniform and beautiful pearly color, and in her entire life she never had one single cavity. It was a remarkable dental record for someone who grew up on a farm in the North Carolina mountains years before available dental and orthodontic care.

Daddy also had beautiful teeth. He was also proud of his. He could take them out! My father did not share Mama's dental DNA. His teeth apparently started rotting as soon as they came in. Born in 1901, he had, by the time he was a teenager, a mouth full of little stubs he described as looking like tree stumps after a forest fire.

At age eighteen, Daddy somehow got to a dentist for the first time. The dentist took one look at his mouth and immediately set in to pull what was left of his tooth stumps. He was then fitted with full upper and lower plates that he wore for the rest of his life.

Daddy was totally comfortable with his false teeth. In no

time, they were more familiar and much more comfortable than when he had real ones. He never took them out except to clean them. He always slept with his teeth in, and almost no one ever saw him without them through the course of his life.

The story was that even Mama did not know he had false teeth when she married him. She also did not know that he had a long habit of chewing tobacco.

Shortly after they were married, they moved into the little house on Plott Creek Road. As soon as they got there, Helen, the milk cow, became a member of the family. Daddy would come home from work at the bank, change his clothes, and go out to milk the cow.

What Mama did not know was that as soon as he was out the door, he would take out his teeth and pop a fat chew of tobacco into his mouth. He gummed on the tobacco while he fed the chickens, milked the cow, and did various other chores to delay his return to the house. On his way back from the barn, he would spit out the tobacco and pop his teeth back into place.

One day about six months after they were married, he went out to milk as usual. Something must have been on his mind that day. When he returned to the house, he had forgotten to take out the tobacco and to put in the teeth. Imagine Mama greeting him at the door. There stood the man she had married, the man she thought she knew, toothless and with brown tobacco oozings outlining his mouth. I am still surprised that she did not run away.

When Joe and I were little, Daddy loved to use the teeth to play with us. He would take them out of his mouth and pretend that they were talking all on their own. We were fascinated by his teeth.

Mama was not. In fact, she hoped that we got her dental genetics rather than his. One of her favorite sayings, every time one of us lost a baby tooth, was, "Oh, I hope you boys did not get your father's teeth!"

Joe and I were equally unlucky in the tooth department, but in two totally different ways.

He got the soft, decaying version of Daddy's teeth. Even his baby teeth decayed. The dentist cauterized the stubs with silver nitrate until he looked pitiful.

My teeth were not that soft, but I had a different set of problems: every single new tooth that I got came in in its own individual direction, without any relationship at all to any of my other past or future teeth. The baby teeth didn't matter, but by the time most of my permanent teeth were in, my mouth was a total mess. I had a hard time closing my lips over all of them.

One day, Daddy was looking at me, and he remarked, "You look just like I did when I was your age. My teeth were just like that, before they all rotted and got pulled out."

Now, I knew another reason he had so much appreciation for his false teeth.

With the advent of fluoride and toothpaste, and with very regular dental visits, my cavities were kept in check. But nothing immediate could be done about the crookedness. Over and over again, however, in eavesdropping on Mama's conversations with Dr. Phil Medford, our dentist, I began to hear the same repeated word: "Braces . . . braces . . . braces."

As far as we knew, braces were a new invention. They were also very expensive. You did not routinely get braces because everyone else had them or because a sheet of paper would not slide between your front teeth. No, braces meant that there were discretionary funds somewhere in the family. So I knew that it was all just talk. I would never have braces.

Things do not always go as you expect them. Daddy had a somewhat distant cousin named Jack Turbyfill. His cousin Jack

was a dentist in Asheville who had become an orthodontist. Maybe they made some kind of deal through the family. I never did
know the details. All that I know was that on the morning of
my thirteenth birthday, I was greeted with a surprise announcement at the breakfast table: "Happy birthday! Guess what? You
are going to get a wonderful birthday present." Mama was the
smiling announcer. "We have arranged for you to get braces for
your birthday!"

It was not in this lifetime what I wanted to hear. By now, I
knew all I needed to know about braces. There were two kids in
my classes at school who had braces, and I wanted nothing at all
to do with what I saw them in the process of enduring.

First, there was Jimmy Hogge. Jimmy Hogge was probably
the most oral child I had ever known in my life. Back in kindergarten, he was always being reprimanded for having several fingers in his mouth at once. By the time we were in the second
grade, he could play "The Flight of the Bumblebee" on his teeth.
He simply could not keep his hands out of his mouth.

It was a popular thing in that day for boys to have watch
chains. None of us had pocket watches, but we had various things
on our watch chains, from rabbit's feet to pocketknives. (Yes, everyone had a pocketknife at school!)

One day, Jimmy Hogge was playing with his watch chain in
his mouth. He was biting the end of it and popping the little clasp
open and shut with his fingernail. All of a sudden, we heard him
gasp and go, "Uuuuh!" The little clasp on the end of the watch
chain had slipped out of his finger grip and closed around the
wire connecting the braces on his two front teeth. He was stuck!

Mrs. Gussie Palmer, our teacher, sent him to call his mother and tell her what had happened. When he got back from the
school telephone, he was crying. Not only did his mother refuse
to come to school to get him, she vowed that she would not take

him back to the orthodontist until his next appointment time came around. For the coming week, that boy came to school each day with a watch chain hanging out of his mouth.

The other classmate with braces was Amelia Gibson. I am sure that when Dr. Turbyfill first looked into Amelia Gibson's mouth, he silently thanked God that the mortgage payments would now surely be paid! She had the biggest and most numerous set of teeth any child had ever carried to Hazelwood School. After her first appointment, she told all of us that four of her teeth had to be pulled just to give the others a possible chance of being forced into straight lines.

Since my birthday came on the first day of June, school was now out for the summer. It was not many days until I climbed into the car with Mama and we made the twenty-seven-mile drive to Asheville to meet Dr. Turbyfill. Daddy was not going. His contribution to the trip was to declare that the whole business I was about to go through was not just about straight teeth. He declared, "Just think of it as part of your total education." I was not impressed.

Dr. Jack Turbyfill was a short man with a kind and friendly voice. His office was on the second floor of the Flatiron Building in downtown Asheville, just across side streets from Ivey's Department Store on one side and Woolworth's on the other. Mama filled out all the papers and answered all the questions for me. Finally, it was time for me to go into the actual working part of the office.

There was nothing at all to going to the orthodontist. There were no shots to numb pain, no screeching sound of drills, no burning smell of drilled teeth. All they did was take a set of x-rays (painless), then take impressions of my upper and lower teeth (painless but slightly annoying). Then the appointment was over. We were promised that Dr. Turbyfill would "make a plan of action" and that I would be under way with the next appointment.

It was not two weeks later that we went back to Asheville. I actually looked forward to the trip. On the last trip, we had gone to eat lunch at the S&W Cafeteria after the appointment, and my hope was that we might again get to go to this favorite place. No matter what, there would be a side trip to Woolworth's before the day was over.

I was somewhat afraid that this second appointment would be very different from the first and that I would begin to discover that pain was involved with orthodontics. It was not so. Dr. Turbyfill worked on my mouth and put the bands on all of my lower teeth. Then he added wires to the bands and did a lot of tightening and twisting of the wires. It was actually quite entertaining. There were times when there were ends of long wires hanging out of my mouth before they were trimmed off. It was like putting new strings on a guitar in my mouth.

When the appointment was finished, Mama suggested eating at the S&W Cafeteria, my favorite place. We headed there and splurged on deviled crab. Then we started for home.

That night, I discovered why main-line dentists choose to specialize in orthodontics. Nothing that they do to you actually hurts in the office. It is about two or three hours later, when you are safely back at home with your family, that it begins to hurt.

By the time we were back at home, my mouth was throbbing. Every one of my lower teeth was in a battle for life and death with the next one. The whole assembly was locked in battle. It was a feeling of tension on the edge of explosion.

Mama asked a very meaningless question: "What would you like for supper?"

It was all I could do to answer, "Soup, and no kind that has anything in it that needs to be chewed."

In a few days, all the soreness was gone.

At the next appointment, I got bands on my top teeth, and the entire project was under way. The pattern was a consistent one. We would go to Asheville for the appointment. Dr. Turbyfill would adjust all the wires and put on some new ones. My mouth would be sore for several days. Then it was waiting until the next appointment came. Soon, the summer was coming to an end and school was about to start. This was when Mama went into a panic.

I still remember her report to Daddy at supper one night after my appointment that day with Dr. Turbyfill: "Oh, Joe, I don't know what we are going to do. School is starting next week." (At this time, Mama was teaching second grade at Hazelwood School, and her year was about to begin.) "Dr. Turbyfill's appointment person says that she just cannot make every child's appointment an hour after school is out. She says that it is normal for children to get to leave school to come in for their appointments. How are we going to do this? You have to work, and I will be at school. How are we going to manage?"

Daddy answered almost a little too quickly. "Give me a day to think about it, and I am sure I can come up with a plan." For the night, the conversation was over.

The next night at the supper table, Daddy's concocted plan rolled out. "I have been talking to some of the other parents whose children go to Dr. Turbyfill. Here's the idea that I have: the Trailways bus leaves Waynesville at seven fifty-five in the morning, headed to Asheville. It's a slow route—the one that goes over through Bethel, then Canton, then on to Candler and Enka and through West Asheville to Asheville. It is supposed to get to Asheville at five minutes after nine.

"Here's what we can do: you can put him on the bus at seven fifty-five on your way to school. Make his appointment for about nine-fifteen or nine-thirty. He'll be out of there in no time. The bus coming back from Asheville leaves there at eleven o'clock.

It gets back here at ten after twelve. I can meet him at the bus station at my lunchtime and take him to school from there. The appointment will be done, and he will only miss a half-day of school. How about that for a plan? And remember what I said when we started all of this? It will be a part of his education."

Mama did not know what to say. I thought the plan was wonderful. I was thirteen years old, and except for staying at my grandparents' house I had never in my life been far enough from my mother that I could not feel her breath on me. Now, thanks to crooked teeth and Trailways, I was about to have adventures on my own. (I noticed, but Mama did not, that Daddy failed to tell us whether any of the parents with whom he had talked had actually done this with their own children. I discovered later that I was the first!)

A couple of weeks later, the appointment was made. It was to be at nine-thirty on a Thursday morning. Mama thought the later time would be good in case the bus was late or I was slow getting from the station on Coxe Avenue up to the Flatiron Building.

Early that morning, I was up, bathed, and ready to go. Mama made rude comments about my appearing more interested in the trip than in going to school. I reminded her of what Daddy had said when the braces plan was made: "It will be part of my total education. I won't even really be missing school!"

There were plenty of instructions from Mama on the way to the bus station: "Now, you sit near the front of the bus where the driver can see you. Don't you go way in the back. And get you a seat of your own. If someone tries to come and sit down beside you, you move! And when you get over to Asheville to that bus station there, don't you use the bathroom in the bus station. You hold it until you get to Dr. Turbyfill's office." There was more, but I had stopped listening by then.

I still remember climbing up onto the silver-and-red Trailways bus and looking out the back window at Mama standing beside her car. Watching while the bus drove away, it was a beautiful sight to see her get smaller and smaller and smaller until she simply disappeared. I suddenly felt totally free!

The bus actually got into Asheville a little bit early. I headed up Coxe Avenue, turned the corner onto Patton Avenue, then left up Biltmore Avenue to the Flatiron Building. I was there at nine-fifteen on the nose. They took me in early, and I was rewired, adjusted, and back out of the office before ten o'clock.

Since I knew that I had only a couple of hours before the new version of soreness set in, I decided to go straight to Woolworth's and eat at the lunch counter. They were still serving breakfast, so I had waffles with as much butter and syrup as I wanted. Then I walked up and down every single aisle in the store, looking at and touching everything I wanted to examine to my heart's content.

It was a leisurely stroll back to the bus station early for the eleven o'clock bus back to Waynesville. All went as planned. Daddy was waiting at the bus station, and I was back at school for the entire afternoon. I felt like a free and responsible thirteen-year-old adult.

The next appointment did not work out in exactly the same way.

I never did figure out what happened. When I got to Dr. Turbyfill's office for my next appointment, the office was full of kids when I arrived. I wondered whether his business was booming, or maybe there had been some sort of sickness which caused a lot of makeup appointments.

At any rate, the result was that the entire day was way behind time. I sat there staring at the clock on the wall and listening for my name to be called. When I finally got to go back to one of the chairs, it was already ten-twenty. It took another good ten minutes for Dr. Turbyfill to finish on his other patient and come to me. I could not say a thing with my mouth wide open, but I was silently wishing for quickness. It was not there. He let me go at exactly ten fifty-five.

I ran out of the office, ran down the flight of stairs without waiting for the elevator. I knew there was a shortcut out the back and along Wall Street. Patton Avenue was crossed in an instant, and the bus station was in sight.

What was also in sight was the back end of my Trailways bus leaving for Waynesville, on time for the first time in its life. I had lost the race.

Panting and out of breath, I ran into the station and up to the counter. "I am supposed to be on that bus!" I cried to the ticket agent. "I do not live in Asheville. I live in Waynesville, and I am supposed to be on that bus so my daddy can pick me up and take me to school!"

The Trailways agent was very kind. He simply told me that everything would be okay and that he would be my helper in working things out. Without even needing to look on the schedule, he told me that another bus left for Waynesville at four-ten in the afternoon. It was even a direct bus, stopping only in Canton, and would get me back where I belonged at five o'clock.

After I settled down a little bit, the agent even offered to call my daddy at the bank and tell him exactly what had happened. This suited me just fine, as I did not want to talk with anyone right now.

Once Daddy heard the news, he wanted to talk with me. He was not mad at all. In fact, he seemed to think that everything was a little bit funny. He told me to calm down, go and get something to eat, get a book or a magazine, and he would be waiting for me when the later bus arrived. What a relief!

I counted on my fingers: "Eleven, twelve, one, two, three, four." That seemed like a long time to hang around the bus station, especially since Mama had specifically told me I was not to use the restroom there. I decided to follow Daddy's advice and get food and something to read to fill out the time.

Starting back up Coxe Avenue, the first place I came to was called the Coxe Avenue Newsstand. It was open in the front and had big Coca-Cola coolers right beside the street. There were glass cases filled with candy bars right inside the door. Coke and candy . . . that is food! So I headed inside and bought a bottled Coke and a Baby Ruth (while I could still chew peanuts!).

Daddy had suggested that I get a book or a magazine. The newsstand did not have books, but it was filled with magazines. This was just the place! I started looking at all of them, trying to decide what to buy.

The farther toward the back of the little store you got, the more interesting the magazines were. There were no men in them, and the women were very interestingly clothed, if you could call it that. All of a sudden, the owner of the stand—the very man who had sold me the Coke and candy—saw me back there. He almost shouted, "You, little kid. Get out of there! That is the adult section, and you do not belong there!" He got me so upset and insulted I left without even buying a comic book.

Just across the street from the bus station was the new two-story Sears, Roebuck store. We almost always went there when the family came to Asheville, and I loved the store. The usual frustration was that I was never the shopper. Every time I wanted to stop and look at something, Mama was the one saying, "Don't look at that. You don't need that. We are not going to buy that. Come on."

On this day, I went into Sears, Roebuck in no hurry and with no one to herd me along. The bus did not leave until four o'clock, and it was now only one. For nearly two hours, I inspected every single thing that Sears, Roebuck had to sell, from toilets to truck tires.

On the bus ride back to Waynesville that late afternoon, I knew that I had just had one of the greatest days of my life, and it was all because of a simple, blameless mistake in timing.

After that day, I almost never managed to catch the right bus again! There were plenty of excuses available. "The bus over there was slow, and I got up to the office pretty much after my appointment." "He has so many new patients, it just takes a lot longer than used to take." "Those children from Asheville live so close to the office that they all get there way ahead of me." Not one single one of these excuses was untrue. It was just that when one of them honestly happened, I happened to walk very slowly back down to the bus station, just in case!

At least once every month or two, I had a good full five hours on my own to explore the big city of Asheville without any supervision at all.

Straight across the street from the Flatiron Building was Ivey's Department Store. They had the first escalator in my life. I would go across to Ivey's and simply ride the escalator up and down, up and down, up and down, up and down. One day after riding about six round trips, I came to the bottom and was met by a policeman who had been summoned by the Charles of the Ritz saleslady. Before he could think of a question to ask me, I was out the door and two blocks away. I decided not to shop at Ivey's anymore, if they were going to act like that.

Just up the street from Ivey's was Harry's Pontiac-Cadillac. It was great fun to go into the showroom and look at the new cars, especially the Cadillacs. I would open the doors and sit in the driver's seats, pretending to drive. The salesmen were too polite to limit my looking, as I might be the unknown child of a potential Cadillac customer, and they didn't want to take any chances.

One day, I was walking down Patton Avenue when a large black car pulled over to the curb and the driver rolled down the window. "Hey, kid!" He was talking to me. "Do you know where the liquor store is?"

"Sure," I barked back immediately. Then I proceeded to give the driver a set of directions that would not only not get him to any liquor store in North Carolina but would also assure that I never saw that particular black car ever again.

Two favorite places to check out on my city walks were the Plaza and the Imperial theaters. They were, of course, not operating during my daytime visits, but they had great color posters of all the upcoming attractions. It was great fun to walk back into the recessed entrances behind the ticket windows and look at the advertisements for all the movies that were coming. Once, I remember seeing a poster for a movie called *Hell and High Water*. I could not imagine what that could be about, since those two ideas did not go together at all.

One day, I was walking past the Imperial Theater when there was a great line of people at the ticket window. It did not take me long to realize that it must be spring-break week for Buncombe County schools, and the theater was having special showings for children who were out of school. Without even looking to see what was playing, I got in line and proceeded to buy a ticket.

Once inside, I discovered that I had paid to see a movie called *The Curse of Frankenstein*. Not long after it started, a huge, grotesque monster appeared on the screen. He was reaching toward the audience. The entire house screamed in unison! As the screams continued and intensified, I sat with my eyes closed and my head between my knees, not daring to look at another moment of the movie.

In addition to the Plaza and the Imperial, there was another theater in downtown Asheville. It was on Biltmore Avenue and was called the "Fine Arts." It was a strange place. A lot of the light bulbs that spelled out the name Fine Arts seemed to be perpetually burned out. And all of the windows on the front of the theater were painted solid white. It was hard to see what was playing there, as they never had the names of the movies listed. There were some little, tiny, almost hidden posters behind the ticket booth that seemed to list some movies. They had strange titles like *Foxxes in the Chickkenhouse* and seemed to feature only strangely shaped women. It was a creepy-feeling place.

Biltmore Avenue started on Pack Square, an old part of town with a monument to Zebulon Vance, a two-time governor of North Carolina. It may have once been a nice part of town, but now it was mostly beer joints and pawnshops.

I loved the pawnshops, especially Finkelstein's. They sold wonderful knives and harmonicas. I figured it must be dangerous to play the harmonica, since they were displayed right above the switchblade knives.

Over a two-year period of time, I came to know every street and corner of downtown Asheville, from the Grove Arcade building to Beaucatcher Tunnel. Crooked teeth had made me a real man of the world.

One of the saddest days from my adolescent memory was that day when Dr. Turbyfill made the announcement, "Well, you are finished now. I have done all I can do with you. As long as you wear your retainer regularly, you have no need to come back!" The fun was over.

At age sixteen, I got my driver's license. The first time we went to Asheville after that, Mama agreed to let me drive. She was totally amazed that I got around the city so easily and seemed to know how to go directly from place to place. When she commented on it, I complimented her: "Oh, Mama, you have always been so clear in describing Asheville from your days in teachers college here. I learned from listening to you!"

I think now about the spring of that year when the school annuals arrived. As soon as I got home with mine, Mama wanted to look at it. She went, of course, directly to the class photographs. There I was, smiling, with both rows of straight, brace-free teeth glowing.

"Oh, look at you!" she smiled. "Look at how nice you look! Remember before you got the braces, and you didn't even want to have them? Well, look at that picture. What do you have to say now about having your teeth straightened?"

I smiled back at her. "I'm glad I did it. You see, I always tried to remember what my daddy said that day when I first went over there."

"I don't remember," she said, opening the door.

"He said, 'Son, just think of it as part of your education.' And that is what got me through all the pain and suffering of the whole thing."

Chapter 19

THE NEW OLD CAR

When Mama and Daddy met, Mama had never even ridden in a car. She grew up on a homesteading farm where there were no powered vehicles of any kind. Her father never learned to drive in all of her growing-up years.

She had ridden the train to college and back. For four years, she walked to and from the school where she taught. Not until she met Daddy did she ever get into the first car that ever carried her. She was twenty-five years old at the time.

Needless to say, when she and Daddy got married and started their family, it was a one-car family. There was Daddy, Mama, Joe, and me—and the 1936 black Plymouth. Daddy was the driver. That is the way the world was made, not only for our family but for a predominance of post–World War II American households. A car was a possession of prized luxury, and there were not a lot of them to casually pass around.

When I was in the second grade and Joe was old enough to start to church-basement kindergarten, Mama, who had taken an eight-year hiatus from teaching to have us, decided that it was time for her to go back to the classroom. Daddy agreed, with one condition: she needed to learn to drive.

She objected, "One driver is enough for any family. We have one car, and only one person can drive it at a time. We are always going places together, so there is no need for me to learn to drive."

She lost the argument, and with Daddy as the teacher and the additional coaching of two little boys in the backseat, she perilously learned to drive the 1948 Plymouth.

As soon as she had her driver's license, Daddy started the campaign: "Why don't we get another car?"

"What's wrong with that car?" Mama objected. "We just got it two years ago, and you know Harry will be bringing us another one when we need it." Daddy's brother, our uncle Harry, was a Chrysler-Plymouth dealer in Leaksville, North Carolina. Every few years, he would show up at our house for Christmas with a new car he had decided Daddy was going to buy. It was always the Plymouth that was so profoundly ugly he knew no one would buy it, and he had to get rid of it some way.

"I do know that," Daddy countered. "I am talking about a second car so that we can each have one to drive. Harry can get us a good used car, or we could just keep this one and add a new one when he has one for us."

Mama did not even argue. She simply walked out of the room and closed the door, a little too loudly, behind her. This was bad. If she had argued, there would have been a chance. But if no one will even start to argue with you, how do you have any possibility of winning the fight in the end?

Daddy did not give up. Every time he had a chance, he brought up the idea of the second car.

"It would actually save us money." This was his best argument. "Now, I am taking you to school every morning and driving back from there to work. 'Doubling back,' I call it, and using more gasoline and wearing out the tires. Then, in the afternoon, I have to leave work and go get you and double back again to take you home and then go back to work and probably have to stay later to make up for leaving to take you home. It makes sense for us to have two cars. I'll call Harry!"

Mama did not budge. "If we waste money and get another car that we don't need, people will talk about us. They will say that I went back to teaching school just so we could show off and buy things that we did not need to start with. Besides, as soon as a family begins to go places in different cars, that is the beginning of the end for them. And I have already called Harry and told him in no uncertain words that we do not need a second car, and that he better not think about getting in on this act!"

It seemed that Daddy had lost the battle, but still he did not give up.

At the end of my sixth-grade year in school, we moved to our new house. Daddy now figured that the "doubling back" business was worse than ever before. He figured it was a total of three more miles each day, which meant fifteen wasted miles each week. This translated into sixty useless miles each month, and finally added up to nearly eight hundred never-to-be-recovered miles in the course of a full year.

Uncle Harry brought us a new Plymouth that year during the Christmas season. Daddy said the new car was a special color called "Monkey Vomit Green," and called it "Mama's car," implying that he would soon have his own car. Uncle Harry drove off, taking our old car with him, along with another threat from Mama.

The argument resurfaced when I turned fifteen and was signed up for driver's training at school: "Lucille, we are about to have three drivers sharing one car. In a couple of years, Joe will learn to drive. I don't see how we can possibly divide one Plymouth four ways."

Mama had stopped arguing at all by now. She just turned her back and walked out of the room every time she heard anything about the second car.

Daddy looked at me and offered, "Son, if we are going to win this battle, it is going to take an end run."

I had no idea what he was talking about.

In the spring of that year, it happened. I had finished my time in driver's training and looked forward to getting my license in a matter of weeks. One afternoon, Daddy had left work and picked up Mama at her school. He had then come by junior high and picked up Joe, and next door at the high school added me. We were on the double-back for home.

We were passing a small used-car lot called Stan Henry's Used Cars. Without even giving a turn signal, Daddy simply pulled off the road and into the front lot of Stan Henry's Used Cars.

"What do you think you are doing right now?" Mama did not have a pleasant look on her face.

"Right now, I'm not doing anything. It is already done!" Daddy kept talking so she did not have a reasonable chance to interrupt. "I have already talked with Stan. He has these cars back in the back that he calls 'go-to-work specials.' They are not anything that you would want to drive a long way out of town, but they will easily get a person to work or to school and back. They are not over a hundred dollars. I am getting one to save us time and money. I will drive it to work while you drive the Plymouth. When Donald gets his license, it will be better to have him getting experience on an old clunker than on your good car. It is done!"

Mama looked at me, and I could not believe the words that I heard coming out of her mouth: "You probably had something to do with this, too, mister! You just get out and stay with him. If you're going to drive the thing, you might as well be in on it."

Daddy and I got out of the car. Mama drove off with Joe watching us out the window.

As soon as she was out of sight, Daddy smiled. "End run! Well, now we are going to have to get a car. She has left us no choice. How else are we going to get home? Let's go talk with Stan."

Stan Henry came out of a little house at the back of the lot and greeted Daddy. "What can I do for you, Joe? I don't expect I can sell you a car, with your brother Harry in the car business."

"Today, you can," Daddy was quick to declare. "This is a special day. We are not in the market for one of Harry's new cars. We are in the mood to buy a second car, a 'go-to-work special.'"

Stan smiled. "I've got a lot of good choices for you. Come on back here to the back of the lot and you can look them all over."

We were led behind the little house to a part of the used-car lot that you did not even see when you pulled in from the street. This was an unpaved part of the lot that backed up against a wooden fence near some trees. There was a line of older cars parked with their back ends almost touching the fence.

Stan smiled at both of us and pointed to the long line of cars. "Here you are, boys, 'go-to-work specials'! You can have any car in this lineup for a hundred dollars or less!"

There were old Hudsons and Studebakers, Packards and Kaisers. More standard brands—the kind you could easily find spare parts for—were long gone from the special lineup.

I knew in a moment why these cars were on an unpaved part of the lot. You could almost hear the oil dripping from under some of them. Had they been out on the pavement, entire streams of leaking oil would have run out in the open, instead of being soaked up by the dirt and gravel on which they were parked.

Daddy went down to the end of the line and sighted along the front of all the cars. He kept looking and studying.

"What are you looking for?" I finally asked.

"Well," he sighed, "at a hundred dollars, I figured we might as well shop by the foot. I was looking to see what the longest car for a hundred dollars might be. Look there—one of them is sticking out farther than the others. Let's go see what it is."

We walked past a half-dozen cars along the line and came to the long car. It was something to look at. It was a long, black Super Chieftain Pontiac.

The Pontiac had a heavy chrome bumper and grille in front. There was a big hood ornament that looked like a plastic amber-colored Indian head. (I would later learn that it lighted up at night when the headlights were turned on.) A wide band of chrome stripes ran back the long engine hood from the ornament to the windshield. On the back of the car, the same chrome stripes ran down the trunk lid to the big back bumper.

The car had a wide sun visor that I later would learn kept you from seeing whether a traffic light was red or green unless you hunkered way down in the seat. And some previous owner had recently painted the Pontiac with a brush. The paint job had been carefully done, with all of the brush strokes running from front to back on the car.

"How much is the Pontiac?" Daddy asked.

"That car is on sale today, Joe," Stan smiled. "You can have that fine Pontiac today for only eighty-five dollars. It's a steal. It is a four-speed Hydromatic straight eight."

I had no idea what he was talking about.

We opened the engine hood and looked at the long, in-line eight-cylinder engine. I could see what "straight eight" meant without asking. It was a huge, long, flat-head, monstrous motor. I still had no idea what "four-speed Hydromatic" meant.

Daddy queried Stan, "There is no oil dipstick in this car. It's missing. How are you supposed to check the oil?"

The answer was quick and seemed studied: "You never need to check the oil in this Pontiac. All you have to do is to put in a quart of thirty-weight each time you fill it up with gas, and you will come out exactly right."

Without any more questions being asked, Daddy handed over eighty-five dollars, filled out some paperwork, and we were a two-car family at last.

I was terribly excited when we got into the big Pontiac to head home. It was a sure thing that I would get to drive this car when I got my license the coming year. Daddy started the engine, and we crept out onto the street and started for home.

"This car sure does have a funny smell," I commented.

"New cars have a smell of their own," Daddy smiled. "That's partly why people like to get a new car, so they can have that new-car smell."

I countered, "This doesn't smell like a new car. This car smells like a whole load of ripe babies got locked up in it on a hot day in the summer. It smells like maybe the babies got out but they all left something behind before they left."

"That's called 'old-car smell.'" Daddy never gave up. "You'll get used to it."

I had more questions to ask. "I figured out what a 'straight eight' is when we looked at the engine. But what is a 'four-speed Hydromatic'?"

Daddy pointed to the floorboard of the Pontiac, down under his own feet. "Look down there, son. What do you see? An accelerator and a brake pedal but no clutch. You don't have to even learn how to work the clutch to drive this fine car. It has a mind of its own when it comes to changing gears. It does the whole thing itself, and it has four gears to choose from."

Now, I began to watch and listen carefully. Daddy could stop and go using only one foot to drive, sure enough. The big Pontiac did have its own mind about changing gears, but it seemed like it couldn't quite make up its mind. In the one block from Uncle Grover's house to Frank and Kathryn Kirkpatrick's house, the Super Chieftain changed gears fourteen times!

Soon, we were nearing home, and Daddy put on the turn signal to head up the steep hill of our driveway. No traffic was coming, so he made a good, fast start up the hill. The Pontiac's engine sounded like we were going full speed, but the big car got slower and slower. We barely made it to the top of the hill.

When we got home, I was surprised that Stan Henry called Daddy to see if we made it. Daddy told him about the trouble the new car had pulling our hill. Stan had quick and simple advice: "Put a big cup of oatmeal down the hole where the transmission fluid goes. That will help it a lot." Daddy did, and it did!

Within a couple of months of our getting the Pontiac, I got my driver's license. I got to practice on the Plymouth. It was, after all, straight drive. Everyone knew that you did not really have a real driver's license unless you took the test in a straight-drive car. Once I had the license, however, the only car they ever seemed to let me drive was the old Pontiac. It was a rare thing and a special event for me to get the other car.

Daddy and I shared the Pontiac fairly well. He drove it to work and home each day. I got to drive it to Methodist Youth

Fellowship at church, to band practice, and sometimes to take my friends David, Bill, and Doug bowling or to a movie.

Less than three years later, my brother, Joe, got his driver's license. Now, the old Pontiac had triple duty to do, and it was three more years older than it had been when we paid the eighty-five dollars for it to begin with.

One evening, Daddy started a new conversation as we sat at the supper table. "Lucille," he started calmly and slowly, "the tires are worn slick on the old Pontiac. It is going to cost me over eighty dollars to buy new tires and have them mounted and balanced and put on that car. That is the same, almost, as what I paid for it. It is time to replace the old thing and get a better car. Three of us are driving it now, and it is just about smack worn out. I think I'll call Harry tonight and see what kind of idea he can come up with to get us in better shape for transportation."

Mama looked straight at him. "You picked out that car and were determined to get it. Now, I just guess that it is good enough for two boys if it is good enough for you. You can just keep it and drive it until the wheels fall off. Besides, every time Harry comes, I tell him that he better not talk with you about two new cars when one good car is all that anyone needs."

He did not argue. From the tone of her voice and the look on Mama's face, he seemed to know that he had to do a little bit of thinking before he could go forward.

I didn't hear anything about the car for several days. Then, one day, he came to me and said, "Son, we are going to have to try another end run. Try to come up with an idea, would you?"

I thought about it day and night, but I simply could not figure out a way to get past Mama so we could end up with a better second car than the old Pontiac.

The following Sunday, we all went to Sunday school and

church as usual. After Sunday dinner, I made a few phone calls, then headed out to the old Pontiac. I was going to pick up my three friends so we could all go bowling together at Mid-Way Lanes, three miles away in Clyde.

As soon as all three of them were in the car, David, Bill, and Doug began to make fun of it. "This car smells worse than a bathroom." "If we wanted to get there today, we should have walked." "You sure couldn't get hurt in this thing unless you fell out of it."

It was fine for me to bad-mouth the Pontiac, but the three of them had no business talking that way about "my" car. I had to defend it. "This is a good car! All of you have ridden a lot of times when you might have been walking if it hadn't been for this car. There's nothing wrong with this good Pontiac. Let me show you how fast it can get us there!"

With that, I showered down on the accelerator pedal, and after the Pontiac made about a half-dozen mind changes about the gear in which it thought it ought to be, it took off with increasing speed out of town and on the three-mile trek to the bowling alley.

"How about that?" Bill commented. "It really will go! Just look at the speedometer. Why, it's over forty. Speed demon!"

I was more annoyed than ever and kept the gas pedal stuck to the floor. The Pontiac got faster and faster. The needle on the crescent-shaped speedometer passed the midpoint. It left fifty-five and on to sixty miles an hour.

Then it became impossible to tell how fast we were going. For some strange reason, the front tires of the Super Chieftain were bouncing, but not in rhythm with one another. As they bounced, the speedometer needle flopped wildly from side to side. You could have chosen any speed you wished, and the needle obliged by passing through it.

All of a sudden, there was a terrific exploding sound that

came from under the hood of the car. It was followed by a *Whack-whack-whack* noise that sounded like someone hitting a railroad rail with a sledgehammer. At the same time, a hissing combination of smoke and steam came up from the engine hood all the way around the perimeter. It was all I could do to get the car steered off the road and stopped on the gravel shoulder and see through the windshield at the same time.

We got out in a cloud of dust, and I realized that I must have slid to a stop in the dirt. We all headed to the front of the car, and I opened the engine hood. When the smoke and steam cleared, we looked at the long, straight-eight flathead engine. In one side of the engine block, there was a big hole where a large piece of cast iron was missing. Something was hanging partially out of the hole that suddenly reminded me of a dog with its tongue sticking out. It was a piston rod! We had totally blown the engine.

Being teenage boys, all we knew to do at a time like that was to burst out in raucous laughter. We did, and continued to laugh until the first tiny bits of reality hit us, the first one being the realization that we all had to walk nearly three miles back into town to get home.

The four of us started walking and trying to hitch a ride at the same time. One of us might have had a chance to get picked up, but whenever a passing driver counted up to four, we watched the car actually speed up to get on past us more quickly. We walked all the way back to town and split up, each of us heading home in a slightly different direction.

As I trudged up our steep driveway to the top of the hill, I was trying to work on the story that would need to be told when I got there. It would need to be especially good to get past Mama.

There was good news as soon as I got to the front of the house. There was no car there. Now, I would have extra time to think.

As soon as I opened the kitchen door to go into the house, the news got even better. I could hear the television running, with baseball sounds coming from the living room. And I could hear my daddy snoring. This meant that Mama was gone and I only needed a story for him. He would think of something to take care of her before she got back home.

I walked into the living room, and Daddy suddenly sat up, blinking and rubbing his eyes. "Oh." He looked surprised. "I didn't know you were home. I didn't hear the car come in."

"Actually"—I chose my words carefully—"the car didn't come in. That's why you didn't hear it."

"What happened? Did you run out of gas?"

"No, there was plenty of gas. The car just stopped for some reason."

He looked mystified. "Just stopped?"

"Yep!" I was getting confident now. "I was taking the boys down to Clyde to the bowling alley, and all of a sudden, for no reason at all, it just stopped! It was past the tractor place right beside that new cemetery. It's sitting right there on the side of the road."

"Well," Daddy mused to the world at large, "maybe this is something we can take advantage of. Come on. Let's go over to Lawrence Leatherwood's house and see if we can borrow his Jeep truck. Your mama's at the church at a circle meeting. Let's try to get this done before she gets home."

I knew very well that he had something in mind. I just could not yet begin to figure out what it might be. At any rate, the afternoon promised to be an interesting one.

We headed across the backyard and through the garden to the Leatherwoods' house. Lawrence was out in his garage workshop piddling. He looked up as Daddy spoke while we entered: "Lawrence, we need to borrow something. Could we borrow your

Jeep truck and a pretty long rope that's strong enough to hang a dead Pontiac?"

"Sure, Joe. What happened?" He was curious.

Daddy grinned a grin familiar to us all. "Maybe it's better that you don't know anything about it. Then you won't be able to answer any questions in court!"

They both laughed understanding laughs at that. I chuckled, pretending to know what was going on.

With the big, coiled rope in the back of the dark green Jeep, I directed Daddy down to Clyde and to where he could see the Pontiac on the side of the road. "There it is!" I repeated uselessly.

He drove just past the Pontiac and pulled off the road in front of it. Then he backed the Jeep up so we would be ready to pull the Pontiac home with the borrowed vehicle.

"Let's look at the engine before we take it to see if we can tell what happened."

I knew what he was going to see, but I had no idea what it would tell him or what was coming next. When the big engine hood went up, Daddy looked, and was I ever surprised at what I heard.

"Oh, my! This is good! This is better than I could have planned it myself! It's an end run for sure. We can use this. You get in and steer, and I'll pull you home. You might want to keep one foot on the brake pedal so you won't hit the back of Lawrence's Jeep if I need to stop in a hurry."

I got into the Pontiac while he tied bowline knots in the rope connecting the back bumper of the Jeep with the front of the big car.

"Here we go!" Daddy shouted out the window as we began to roll slowly out onto the empty pavement.

He circled the new cemetery so we would have an easy way to turn around and head back toward town. We never went over about twenty miles an hour on the way back, and it seemed like it took forever to get home. The tricky part was the hard turn into the driveway and the steep pull up the hill to the house. We made it safely.

Daddy got out of the Jeep and came back to where I was handling the Pontiac. "Let's untie it, and then the two of us can push it right up into its parking place. We're going to put it exactly where it would be if you had driven it home."

We did what he had said. He then took the keys to the dead Pontiac, carried them into the kitchen, and placed them on the cup hook where they always stayed when the car was at home.

Then, with a gleam in his eye, Daddy looked at me and began a litany of instruction: "When your mama gets home from the circle meeting at church, you let me do most of the talking. If you need to talk, you talk about homework and Sunday school and what your friends might be doing. If there is any talking to be done about cars, I will be the one to do it."

I was totally happy with that.

Soon, Mama got home and automatically started cooking our supper. My little brother, Joe, came home from playing with Ronnie Leatherwood. Soon, we were all seated at the table, blessing and then eating Mama's food. Daddy began eating just like it was a normal meal, and for a long time he didn't say anything at all.

Then he asked, "How was the circle meeting?"

"Just like always," Mama answered. "We spent almost all of the time hearing the finance report from last time and talking about whether it is a good idea to put cushions on the pews in church. I think it would be a good idea, but some of the older women think that all the men will sleep more if we make it more comfortable."

Daddy nodded like he was interested and taking it all in.

After the meal was finished, I realized that nothing at all had been said about the car. Daddy was taking a big bite of coconut cream pie when he casually started the comment: "Oh, I almost forgot. Tomorrow is Monday. I have to go over to the west side of Asheville in the morning to appraise a house for a man who wants to get a mortgage at the bank. I really need to get it done and then be back at work by about eleven o'clock. So, Lucille, I better drive the Plymouth. You can drive the Pontiac and take the boys to school."

My own bite of pie was half swallowed just as he said, "You can drive the Pontiac," to Mama. Now, it was totally hung in my throat and would not go either up or down. I thought I was going to choke to death. I let out a big cough.

"Are you all right?" Daddy quickly asked.

"I am fine. Something just went down the wrong way." As I recovered, I pushed back my chair and left the table. "I think I'd better check on my homework and get to bed early," I offered. "Tomorrow is a new week at school."

Mama smiled with approval.

Later in bed, I could not get to sleep. All I could do was toss and turn and think about all the possibilities that had potential for the next day. It was a delicious wakefulness.

The next morning, I got up on time and headed to the kitchen for breakfast. Daddy was already there and was reading the morning paper. Mama was alternately cooking and calling brother Joe to come to eat.

I could hardly bring myself to choke down a bite. I was amazed, watching Daddy eat like it was the most normal thing in the world to do. He finished, took a last drink of coffee, and wiped his mouth. "I'd better get going if I'm going to get back."

With that, he picked up Mama's keys to the Plymouth, headed out the door, got into that car, and was gone. The rest of us finished our breakfast.

"Well, we better go. It takes a little longer in that old car. Get your stuff and meet me out at the car." Mama hated driving the old Pontiac.

I gathered my school books and made my way to the car very slowly. It seemed to me to be an unwise thing to sit in the front seat with Mama. I knew that if I moved slowly, my brother, Joe, would be delighted to grab the front seat.

Mama was waiting in the car when I climbed into the seat directly behind her. That seemed to me to be the place where she was least likely to see my face. I never could keep a straight face when I had to give questions crooked answers. As she put the key into the ignition switch, I put my head down in my lap to try to disappear before what I knew was coming.

Mama turned on the switch, then pushed the starter button on the dash of the Pontiac. The noise was horrible: *Thunk, bunk, dunk-dunk-dunk!* The starter tried desperately to turn over the dead engine.

"What's wrong with it? Why is it making that noise instead of starting?"

I tried to offer a suggestion while ignoring her question: "I think you need to give it some more gas. It sometimes doesn't like to start first thing in the morning."

She pumped the accelerator pedal a few times, then hit the starter button again. *Dunk-dunk-dunk.* It was giving out.

"I think maybe you flooded it," I offered.

Mama was quick to give up on the old car. "Let's get out of this thing and go over to the Leatherwoods'. Maybe Lawrence hasn't gone to work yet, and he can give us a ride to school."

Since Mr. Leatherwood was the superintendent of schools, he was happy to give an even out-of-the-way ride to Mama, who was, after all, one of his schoolteachers. He was just as happy to take Joe and me by the high school on the way.

We were on the way before the question came: "What's wrong with your car, Lucille?"

"It's not my car. Joe took my car today to go over to West Asheville and back. I was supposed to drive that old Pontiac of his. It wouldn't start."

I could see the questioning gleam in his eye as he remembered the Jeep loan and added that to what she said. "Wonder what's wrong with it? It's been running okay, hasn't it?"

"I drove it just yesterday, and it was fine," I volunteered.

It was Mama's turn for a question to Mr. Leatherwood: "Maybe you could come over this afternoon and look at it before Joe gets home?"

The plan was made. Mr. Leatherwood would pick the three of us up at the end of our various school days. Then he would take us home so he could have a diagnostic look at why the car wouldn't start.

I had a hard time paying any attention at all to any of my teachers that day. I knew that somehow Daddy had a big plan going in all of this, but I still hadn't quite figured out exactly what it was.

Afternoon came. We rode home just as we had gotten to school. Mama repeated the request: "Would you mind coming over and just looking at Joe's car?" Mr. Leatherwood was happy to do so.

I pulled the release and opened the long hood uncovering the straight-eight engine. Mr. Leatherwood took one look at the hole in the side of the block with the rod sticking partially out of it.

"Good grief, Lucille! What in the world did you do to Joe's car?"

"I think I flooded it." She remembered what I had told her.

"Flooded it? I think you've drowned it. This car will never run again!" He closed the hood and quickly turned his back and went home.

Mama took a few deep breaths, then walked calmly into the kitchen and began to cook supper. She took her time and fixed a very fine meal.

After the trip to West Asheville made him late to work for the day, Daddy was a little bit late getting home. At last, he came.

Instead of the usual kitchen table, Mama had set the nice china on the dining-room table for dinner. All of this drew no comment from any of us. We simply sat down to eat like this was the most normal thing in the entire world. I had a hard time eating. Daddy ate like he was starving.

We finished all the main courses, and Mama brought out ice cream with chocolate syrup for us each to fix our own dessert. We were slurping away when Daddy finally spoke. "Well, Lucille, I had a nice day today. It was a quick trip over to West Asheville and back, thanks to your car. How did you get along with the Pontiac?"

"Just fine!" Her answer was immediate. "We all got along just fine. But there is one thing I would like to know."

"What's that?" Daddy was smiling.

"With a brother who is in the car business—a brother who could bring you a better car just by your making one telephone call—why, why, why do you insist on continuing to drive that dangerous piece of junk you call a car that is sitting right out there in our driveway? And why do you dare have our boys driving around in that awful and unsafe thing when you could make one telephone call and have a new car tomorrow?"

Daddy did not even attempt to answer the question. He simply got up from the table and walked over to the telephone. He called his brother Harry and spoke only four words to him: "She says it's time."

By the next afternoon, we had a much newer and only slightly used Plymouth, and the Pontiac was forever gone to Betsy Schulhofer's Junkyard. I also knew that if Daddy ever had any idea about using an "end run" on me, whatever it was, he would win.

Chapter 20

IRRATIONAL FEAR

Since my father's parents both died before I was born, I never knew the grandparents on this side of the family. No, whenever grandparents were mentioned, it meant only one thing to Joe and to me: Grandmother and Granddaddy Walker. Through all the years of my growing-up life, we continued to go to visit them all the time.

Granddaddy Walker was a farmer, though by the time I really remember him what he mostly did was walk around looking at the farm. Grandmother continued to work nonstop, through heart attacks and bouts with cancer, until the end of her life.

We went to see them at least once a week. Often, it was Sunday afternoon. Pretty often, it was anytime on Saturday. Sometimes, it was another time of the week, especially in the summer or during a holiday when school was out.

One day, we were getting in the car to go for one of our visits. My little brother, Joe, looked up at Daddy and asked the question: "Why do we go to see Granddaddy and Grandmother so much? We go out there every time we turn around."

Daddy quickly answered, "It's because they don't have a telephone. We have to go see if they're dead. Since they don't have
a telephone, they can't call us and tell us if they are dead. They
could just lie there dead for a week if we didn't go check on them."

Three of us laughed. Mama did not think it was funny.

From then on, every time we started out to see Grandmother
and Granddaddy, my brother, Joe, would make the announcement: "Let's go see if Grandmother is dead! Let's go see if Granddaddy is dead!" Eventually, even Mama chuckled.

I loved going to their house. The farm, which Mama remembered mostly as a place of childhood work, was fascinating to me.
After turning off the paved county road, there was a rough dirt-
and-rock road which ran the last mile to the house. There were
creeks and woods and mountains to climb. Every time we went
there, I would beg Mama, "Let's go up on the mountain. Let's go
up to the big rock and build a fire and cook our supper. Let's go
up to the top and see where the sun goes at night. Let's go up to
the place where you spanked the cow with the pokeberries and
turned it purple!"

After enough begging, Mama would give in. "Okay. Let's go.
But wait a minute until I fix my stick."

She would then go out into the yard of Grandmother's house
and cut a piece of limb off a tree. The limb would be the right size
for a walking stick, but it had to have a good fork in it. She would
trim the forked end until she had a pronged point. That end went
toward the ground as we walked. Mama was scared to death of
snakes!

We would walk along with her probing the trail from side
to side like a blind person checking the way with a white cane.
Suddenly, she would come to an abrupt halt and point the stick
toward a nearby spot on the ground. "There was one right there. I

don't know what kind it was, but it was as big as my arm!"

"When was that, Mama?" I would ask.

"When I was about eight years old," the answer came.

A few steps later, she pointed again, this time at a large, flat rock. "There were two of them right there. One was a blacksnake and one was a rattler. The rattler grabbed the blacksnake by the tail, and then the blacksnake grabbed the rattler by the tail, and then . . . they proceeded to totally eat one another up!"

"Did you see that?" I had to ask.

"No," she sheepishly answered. "But I heard all of them talk about it."

To listen to Mama's commentary, there had been a snake on every square foot of that farm during her lifetime. No matter how many times we went there, I never, ever saw one single snake on my grandparents' farm.

As I got older, my love of the place did not go away. After all, Grandmother not only thought I was cute, she had a strong belief that sugar was a primary food group. When I went there, she would save the extra biscuit dough, roll it out very thin, put a layer of homemade applesauce on it, add more sugar and cinnamon, flip the dough over the applesauce and crimp it with a fork, and fry it in butter in the frying pan. Since the first side soaked up all the butter, she had to add more butter for the second side. Then, once they were done, we ate up the little fried pies with cold, fresh milk from her cow. She called the pies "Rooster Pies." When I asked why, she said that they were shaped like the comb of a rooster. I didn't care what she called them—I loved them.

By the time I got to junior high school, I began to seriously try to figure out my mama. One day, I came home from school in the eighth grade and made a terrible mistake. As we ate supper, I said to Mama, "We read about you at school today."

"Really?" This gave her a little smile on her face. "How did you read about me at school?"

"You are in one of our school books. It is as clear as day that it is you."

"Which book are you talking about? I don't think I could be in a school book." She was curious now.

I could not stop. "It was our health book. We were reading the chapter called 'Mental Health.' You are in there. It's about the snakes. You have what the book calls an 'irrational fear' of snakes. You are not normal!"

I definitely should not have said that, especially the last part. Mama was onto me in a flash. "I will tell you about irrational fear, mister! Irrational fear is always something someone else has. If *you* are afraid of something, it makes more sense to you than anything in the world! And someday, something is going to happen to show you all about that!" She turned and walked out of the kitchen.

Eventually, I turned sixteen. In North Carolina, when we turned sixteen years old, there was a particular ritual that had to be completed by every male. If you were a male (I don't know about females), on the day when you turned sixteen, you presented yourself at the nearest office of the Division of Motor Vehicles. You waited patiently until your turn came, then you turned in your brain, and they gave you your driver's license. (They kept your brain for a long time after that because, at age sixteen, you had little use for it anyway.)

My birthday came on the first day of June. This meant that I got my new driver's license at the beginning of the summer when I finished the tenth grade in high school. The whole summer was ahead of me as a new driver.

The frustrating thing was that my parents did not believe

in meaningless, indiscriminate, pointless, endless, destination-less driving around. So it was a very difficult thing to actually get to drive a family vehicle that summer. (The actual concept of a sixteen-year-old having a car of his own had not been invented.)

However, as the summer rolled on, I learned a wonderful trick that always worked. All I had to do was get a sad look on my face, go up to my mama, and whine, "I miss my grandparents. Would it be okay for me to go to see Grandmother and Grand-daddy?" My mother could not resist. Out came the keys and usually an offer for gas money.

Since there was no telephone at Grandmother's house, how did they know? How did they know when I got there? How did they know when I left? How did they know what myriad routes I discovered on the long way there and back?

One day, still in June, I had secured the keys to Mama's car and was out for a visit. I went early in the day so Grandmother would have ample opportunities to feed me. Her belief in sugar as a food group continued. There was a new round of Rooster Pies, this time with peach filling.

After a while, Granddaddy came into the kitchen. He ate one of the little fried pies, then said to me, "Let's go for a walk up around the barn. There are some little grafted trees I have up there. They are doing pretty well, but I still like to keep a good check on them."

We took off. The big barn was only a couple of hundred yards up the hill from the house. He and I walked up there and checked out the trees. He loved to graft fruit trees so there were several varieties on a single tree. He checked out a few more things around the barn, then we started back down the dirt path to the house.

About halfway back, we were almost startled when a little blacksnake darted from one side of the worn path across toward the other side. It stopped right in front of us as if it had just no-ticed us and was checking us out. Granddaddy reached down, and before the little snake knew what was happening, he picked it up.

It was a young and small snake—a teenage snake, a little training snake. It was no larger than your finger and not much over a foot long, if that.

"Look at this little fella," Granddaddy mused. "I am going to put him in the corncrib. There, he can catch mice and grow up to be a good rat eater. He will be happy up there."

I broke in with a new idea. "May I have the snake?" I heard myself say almost before I thought about what I was saying.

"What do you want with a blacksnake?" he wondered to me.

"I want to take it to my mama!" was the quick answer.

Granddaddy chuckled. "I will give you this snake under one condition: you do not ever tell her that I had anything at all to do with it!"

I swore up and down that I was good at keeping secrets. Granddaddy then walked back up to the barn and got a towsack. He put the snake in the towsack and tied a length of grass string around the top. He handed the wiggling sack to me.

The sack was soon placed in the trunk of my mama's car. Soon, I was on the way home, working on my presentation plan in my mind all the way.

Once back at home, I went in the house and left the little snake in the car. I needed to think for a little while to figure all of this out. Some time passed with no plan yet made, so I decided to go back out to the car and check on the snake. When I opened the trunk of the Plymouth, there was the sack. It was flat and empty, with the string wiggled off the end of it. The snake was gone!

I searched the trunk of the car, behind the spare and all over from corner to corner. I crawled under the car and looked in the wheel wells and along behind the rocker panels. Next was the in-side of the car, from under the seats to under the dashboard. Last was under the engine hood, looking everywhere, even to taking the top off the air cleaner. There was no snake. It was simply gone.

Being sixteen years old, within about fifteen minutes, I forgot all about the snake.

About two days later, it was time for us to go for a visit to see if my grandparents were dead. On this day, Mama was going, I was going, my brother, Joe, was going. Daddy thought up some-thing he had to do. He often did that these days.

We headed out early in the morning. Grandmother made Rooster Pies. We visited and finally stayed on through the mid-day meal. About two in the afternoon, it was determined to be time to go home. We told Grandmother and Granddaddy good-bye like we would never see them again and promised to be back before a week had passed.

Mama was driving on the way home. I was riding beside her in the front seat. Joe was in the backseat where little brothers be-longed. We were about halfway home on the sixteen-mile trip when it happened. We had reached a part of the road everyone called "the Narrows," a section of the old road that curved back and forth high above the Pigeon River. Mama was carefully driv-ing through these curves when, all of a sudden, I saw the snake.

On the Plymouth, the defroster came out through vents that ran all the way along the base of the windshield. Right in front of me, at the right-hand end of the defroster vents, up popped the snake. Its little head came up first, looking around, with its tongue feeling the air. *There you are!* I said silently to myself, won-dering where the little creature had been for the past two days.

I quietly watched as the little snake kept coming up out of the vent. It was traveling along the base of the windshield from right to left, right along the track toward my mama. I kept wondering how snakes move the way they do, almost flowing along with no legs at all. I watched, just like the snake and I had a secret between us, as the little fellow glided along the base of the windshield until its little tail popped out of the vent in front of me. This meant that its head was directly in front of Mama.

My mother was a very nervous driver. Her vision was focused about thirty yards down the road in front of us. Between her eyes and her focal point on the road, she saw nothing. I began to fear that she was going to miss the snake. I was afraid that it would go all the way across the car and disappear down into the defroster vent on the other side and she would never get to see it. I did not want to be the one to point it out to her. . . . No, I just did not want her to miss the experience.

At about that time, we started around the last big curve on this part of the road. Just as we were entering the curve, it started to sprinkle rain. To be sure that she was safe, Mama reached down and turned on the windshield wipers.

Later on, I tried to figure out exactly what happened next. It occurred to me that humans have very large brains, and that, with those large brains, humans would easily realize that between the little blacksnake and the windshield wiper there was a solid tempered-glass windshield. But snakes have very small brains, and this was a very small snake. It did not know this.

The moment the wiper went *Swoorp!* across the windshield, the little snake emitted an amazing *Hssss!* and drew back as if to strike at the offending wiper. When it drew back, the back of its head almost smacked Mama right in the mouth! She screamed, her arms went straight and stiff, still holding the steering wheel, and it did not matter where the road went because we were not going there!

The Plymouth accelerated in a straight line right off the side of the road and stood on its nose in the ditch. By the time it had stopped, Mama had grabbed the door handle, flung open the door, and abandoned her children! She cleared the centerline in the road in the first leap and Albert McCracken's pasture fence with the next. She was running away from the snake.

And she had totally lost her punctuation! "Run run there's a snake there's a snake run get out of the car run run!"

At about this time, my little brother, Joe, had gathered himself up out of the floorboard of the backseat and pulled himself up over the back of the front seat. He was looking at me and asking over and over again, "What's happening? What's happening?" I pointed, and he watched as the little snake finished its trip across the dashboard, dropped out the open door, and happily started its way back home.

Gradually, she got herself under control and started back toward the car. I supposed that her intention was to at least try to save us. She said without pause, "Get out of the car get out now run listen to me run!"

She was coming across the road now. When she was about an arm's length from the car, I made a terrible mistake: I laughed at her.

She flushed red and pulled a loaded finger on me! With her finger almost in my face, I heard not unfamiliar words: "Something is going to get you, something is going to get you!"

When we were finally pulled out of the ditch and got safely home, I discovered that "something" had a name. It was called "my daddy."

The ride home had been marked by deep silence. The remainder of the afternoon at home was dominated by the same loud silence. Finally, I heard Daddy's car come in the driveway and knew that something was surely about to happen now. When he came in the kitchen door, Mama looked straight at him and silently jerked her head toward their bedroom. His face dropped all expression as he followed.

As soon as they were behind the closed door, there came from there sounds like wild animals scrapping. There was a high-pitched, "*Blooerooeringhoo . . . ghlibberooniner . . . blobberkingoolero . . .*" It went on and on, only occasionally interrupted by a low-pitched, "*Whaaeerr? Noerooww?*" With not a single understandable word, the meaning of these sounds was totally and absolutely clear: there would not be a happy ending to this day!

Finally, Daddy emerged from the closed room. He looked at me and in a low voice said, "Let's go into your room!"

He led the way so quickly that I had to move fast to keep up with him. We barely made it into my bedroom and got the door closed when he fell on the floor laughing his head off! All he could do was to moan, over and over again, "I wish I had been there! I wish I had been there!"

After he had worn himself out laughing, he looked at me and said, "There is one little problem: I am married to her. And she made me promise that I would punish you for everything that happened today and everything she imagines led up to it, whatever that was." He went on, "But I think I might have a deal for you. Give me your new driver's license."

"No!" I moaned. "Not that. I just got it. It's still early in the summer. Please don't take my driver's license away while school is out for summer vacation."

"Don't worry so much," he offered. "I thought about what I was doing. Just listen. I told your mama that I would take your new driver's license away from you one day for every inch long the snake was. But you get to tell me—how long was it?"

Since I had traded my brain for the driver's license to begin with, I did not have usable access to it at this moment. I thought, however, that I did. I chuckled at the idea that offered itself. "I can't tell you how *long* it was. It was so little I can only tell you how *short* it was. That little snake was so short, it was impossible to measure. If you could measure it, it would probably have negative length. It was so little maybe it wasn't even a snake. Maybe it was just a shadow on the windshield. It had no length. I cannot tell you how *long* it was!"

Daddy got an expression on his face that was somehow a frown and a grin at the same time. "That is truly too bad," he started. "Your mama said that I should ask you first, but if you did not know how long the snake was, she did!"

When the day was over, I had lost my driver's license *fifty-four days* over a preadolescent snake!

The summer rolled on. I walked or begged rides everywhere. Finally, just before school started back, my license was returned, and the snake business was mostly forgotten.

One night in September, my three best friends—David Morgan, Bill McInvaille, and Doug Robertson—were over at our house for supper. Mama had made spaghetti, and the four of us were having a good evening eating as much of it as we could. We were talking about dreams and making plans about all the things we wanted to do. One idea involved an appeal to Mama. We needed to use her car to go to a new movie that was in town.

David was the boldest one of us, so he took her on. "Mrs. Davis," he began his plea, "there is a new movie in town that everyone we know has already been to see."

She jumped right on him. "David, if it is new, how has everybody already been to see it?"

He kept on, "Because it is so good that it has been sold out ever since it got to the Strand Theatre. It has just now been here long enough so that we might have a chance to get in. Could Donald possibly use your car one night so that the four of us could all go to the movie? It really is a good one. Even some of our teachers have been talking about it."

"Well, David"—Mama kind of liked to play with him—"what is the name of this great movie?"

"It is called Alfred Hitchcock's *Psycho*. It really is supposed to be good."

"Boys"—Mama was talking to all of us now—"that movie will scare you. I have heard about it. It is not fit for you to go to!"

That made us even more determined. I took over. "It will not scare us. We are not the ones who have irrational fear. Besides, it is a 'thought' movie—*Psycho*, a thought movie. You do want us to think, don't you?"

Not a one of us saw the little, subtle smile on Mama's face as she said, "Well, boys, sure you can have the car. I don't want you to keep from thinking. I think you will all enjoy Mr. Hitchcock's 'thought' movie. When do you want to go?"

"Maybe tomorrow night," I answered for us all without even asking the others.

At school the next day, we got our plans together, and at about six-fifteen that evening, I started out in the car to pick up all the boys so we would not be late to get good seats for the seven o'clock show of *Psycho*.

My first stop was to get Doug Robertson. Doug lived on Keller Street, off Leatherwood Street behind the Waynevilla Motor Court. The Waynevilla was a collection of little cabins once very nice but now somewhat decrepit, though still in business. If we saw a car there, we usually made a joke about someone who didn't know any better than to stay there. Especially from the backside, there was something creepy about it.

After Doug, I headed over to Boundary Street to get Bill Mc-Invaille. Bill and his half-sister, Sarah Ann, lived in part of the old Redmond house. It was a huge, old house where the Redmonds were seldom home. The house itself gave me the creeps. I did not even like to go up to the door to get Bill. I would break my mama's rule and sit in the car and blow the horn for him to come out. He was used to the place.

Last of all, I went to pick up David Morgan on Pigeon Road. David lived with various aunts and uncles and his grandmother. Whenever you got out of the car at David's house, you could look up at the window of the house on the hill and see Grandma rocking in her rocking chair.

Now, we were all collected. We headed into town and parked right on Main Street, got our tickets at the Strand, and headed inside for the great wonder of *Psycho*.

As soon as the movie started, I knew why Mama did not want us to see it. Right there, in front of all the viewing world to see, was beautiful Janet Leigh—Marion Crane in the movie—sitting on a bed in a hotel room with her boyfriend. And she was in her underwear! The fact that it was very decent underwear and covered up more than most public bathing suits did nothing to blunt our excitement. It was, after all, technically underwear!

This is what Mama thought was going to scare us? This was great. The four of us started giggling immediately. This really was going to be a "thought" movie!

It got better by the second. Marion Crane, the main character, was going to run away with her boyfriend. She had even stolen the money to make this all possible. But she chickened out and turned around to go back to where she belonged. What made it a story was that she turned around too late and had to stop for the night on the way back home.

That is when the movie got funny! She stopped at a place called the Bates Motel, and it looked almost exactly like the backside of the Waynevilla Motor Court across Leatherwood Street from Doug Robertson's house! We started poking at one another and laughing. "Look there, Doug. Back there is your house. If you had been out there on that night, you might have seen her!" David suggested. We all punched and laughed out loud.

All around us, people were looking at us. "Shhh! Shhh!" they whooshed at us. We heard a lady whisper, "It is not funny! If you boys can't be serious, why don't you go out in the lobby and leave the rest of us alone?" We tried to behave after that, but it was not easy.

Marion Crane could not find anyone at the Bates Motel to give her a key. She had to go up to a big house on the hill above the motel. As the camera started to show the old house, it made all of us think of the old Redmond house where Bill lived on Boundary Street. We started giggling again. "Maybe we are all going to be in this movie," Bill suggested now. "The next thing we know, David, we will be going up to your house and we'll see Ma in her rocking chair!" We were out of control.

Once in a room at the Bates Motel, Marion Crane totally possessed us. She proceeded to get ready to take a shower. After the underwear scene at the beginning of the movie, the shower scene made promises we could hardly entertain. *After all, you have to take it all off to take a shower,* we thought. She stepped into the shower and turned on the water. We waited to see what we could see!

At that moment, the fun ended. For months after that moment, I awakened in the middle of the night crying amid nightmare images of red blood, red blood, red blood streaming down the shower curtain and wall and circling toward the drain—and it was a black-and-white movie!

The rest of the time in the theater the four of us spent with our eyes closed and our heads down between our knees. I discovered that even fingers in your ears did not stop the incessant and repeated, *Weeooo, weeooo, weeooo,* of the endlessly unchanging sound track, which went on and on without any words being spoken for long minutes in the film.

After what seemed like forever, I decided it was time to take a look to see if things had gotten any better. I picked the wrong time. Just as I opened my eyes, what was left of Grandma spun around in her rocking chair! The entire theater screamed!

The real genius of Alfred Hitchcock was that he did not actually show you anything. No, he simply led you right up to the edge of terror and then let you do all the work in your own mind. The problem with that is singular: when the movie is over, your mind goes home with you!

David and Bill and Doug and I left the theater along with everyone else who had survived *Psycho* . . . for now. We got in the car, which was parked right out in the light on Main Street, and started home.

First off, I headed out to Keller Street to drop Doug off at his house. When we got there, I turned around in the driveway, then pulled up to the sidewalk in front of the house. Doug just sat there. After a couple of quiet minutes, I said, "Aren't you going to go in your house?"

The reply was quick and unstudied: "Somebody walk up to the door with me."

No explanation was needed. We knew he was not about to get out of the car alone. Finally, Bill got out and walked with Doug up to the dark door of the house. Everything looked fine until Doug unlocked the door and started to go inside. At that moment, Bill grabbed him by the arm and pulled him back out on the stoop. We could hear him all the way out to the car: "Don't you leave me out here by myself." At that point, both of them came back down the sidewalk and got back in the car.

I tried to drive over toward Boundary Street to deliver Bill to his home at the old Redmond house. As soon as we turned up the hill and he saw the house, he said, "Can I just go home with you?"

There was a brief attempt to take David home. But when we turned in the driveway and saw Grandma sitting up there through the window, rocking in her rocking chair, I put the car in reverse and backed out of there fast!

We proceeded to simply go to my house, where we would all spend the night together and figure out how to get everybody back home in the morning.

At our house, there was a large double garage that was part of the house itself. You could drive the car into the garage, get out, and go straight into the kitchen without going back outside. At the moment, this seemed like a very good idea.

I pulled the car up to the garage, and, with the headlights shining brightly inside, we looked all around to be sure that no one was hiding in there. Then, with two of the boys keeping their eyes on the open garage door for security, I slowly turned the car around so we could back inside and be sure that no one was sneaking in behind us.

Once in the garage, we jumped out of the car, slammed the big door down, and locked it. Then we went quickly inside the house and locked the never-locked kitchen door behind us. Without even needing to talk about it, we went all around the house and made sure that every door was securely locked. These doors had not been locked since we had moved in four years before.

There were plenty of bedrooms and plenty of beds in that house. But on this night, four sixteen-year-old boys pulled blankets and pillows out of the hall closet, built a fire in the fireplace (it was the middle of summer), and made a community bed on the living-room floor, where we could sleep touching one another to be sure that nothing got any of us in the night.

The next morning, we were still on the floor, finally asleep, when Mama came through the room. "Well, boys, I didn't know you were all here. I will go in the kitchen and fix breakfast for everybody while you all go take a shower!"

That did it. I knew that I would stay dirty and stink for the rest of my life before I got into a bathtub that had a shower curtain around it. That morning, for the first time in years, four teenage boys took turns taking tub baths in the big bathroom, each bathing while the other three guarded the door for safety.

Finally, we got to the kitchen. It smelled so good in there. Mama had made fresh coffee and now was getting ready to make French toast for all of us. There was a loaf of homemade bread on the countertop, and a big and sharp butcher knife resting beside the bread. Mama picked up the knife, tested its sharpness with her thumb, and began to hack at the bread.

Every one of us had bulging eyes and sweaty lips. "Will you please put that knife away?" It was David who was speaking. "Please . . . now!" The other three of us were nodding and hoping that the knife would disappear. It looked menacing even as my own mama held it.

"What in the world is the matter with you boys?" she smiled.

"I will tell you what." I was now the spokesman. "After that movie that you made us go see, that knife could kill any ten snakes that you have ever even dreamed of, that's what!"

In that moment, I realized that we had all learned about irrational fear. Like Mama said years before, "Irrational fear is always something that someone else has. If *you* are scared of something, it does not matter what it is, it makes more sense to you than anything in the whole world!"